FOCUS
on Suzuki Piano

creative and effective ideas for teachers and parents

by Mary Craig Powell

Design: Aean Pinheiro

Copyright © 1988 Summy-Birchard Music
division of Summy-Birchard Music Inc.
Exclusive print rights administered by Alfred Publishing Co., Inc.
All rights reserved   Printed in USA

ISBN-10: 0-87487-582-X
ISBN-13: 978-0-87487-582-9

The Suzuki name, logo and wheel device
are trademarks of Dr. Shinichi Suzuki
used under exclusive license by Summy-Bichard, Inc.

Table of Contents

Mary Craig Powell

Mary Craig Powell received her baccalaureate degree *Magna Cum Laude* from East Carolina University, Greenville, North Carolina. Her Master of Music in Piano Performance is from Wichita State University in Kansas.

She has taught at colleges in North and South Carolina and Illinois, and currently offers Suzuki teacher training and student lessons at Capital University in Columbus, Ohio. Interest in Suzuki piano pedagogy began while her sons were studying Suzuki violin in the early 1970s. Already known as a fine teacher, her reputation grew to international proportions when she based her instruction on the Suzuki philosophy. Her young students are consistent winners in auditions and competitions. She communicates her high standards and common sense approach to teachers and students' parents with lectures and demonstrations at workshops and conferences throughout the world.

She has further served the Suzuki movement through elective offices in the Suzuki Association of the Americas and the Suzuki Association of Ohio.

Dedication

To my wonderful sons, John and Robert,
with whom my love of the Suzuki method began.

Preface

During the past few years it has been exciting to watch the area of Suzuki piano develop. Through workshops, institutes,and teacher development courses, parents and teachers have been able to grow and improve their skills in an unprecedented way. I have seen their craving for more information and techniques, and it is my hope that *Focus on Suzuki Piano* will be a contribution in those areas and the growth of the remarkable Suzuki movement.

This book is the result of an effort to record and preserve many of the ideas and techniques I have used over a period of years as I adapted my teaching to the Suzuki philosophy. It has been compiled from articles that first appeared in *Suzuki World* magazine betwen 1982 and 1987. Although a connecting philosophy weaves its way throughout the book, each chapter is complete in itself. Thus, it may be read in whatever order the reader wishes. By no means does it represent an examination of all aspects of Suzuki piano, nor is it all I have to offer on the subject. I have more to write.

Mary Craig Powell

Clarification

Because the English language lacks a singular pronoun which can refer to either "he" or "she," for the sake of clarity or consistency we have used "he" to mean the student and "she," the teacher throughout the book. In a few instances when the author is referring to a particular female student, "she" is used to refer to the student, but in these rare instances, it is obvious that the reference is to the student, not the teacher.

Although the Suzuki "parent" does not need to be the mother, "mother" is used to refer to that adult who accompanies the child to the lesson and is responsible for the supervision of the listening and practice at home.

Acknowledgments

It all began with a phone call. Lorraine and Reginald Fink were asking me to become piano editor of their newly-formed magazine, *Suzuki World*. It was too exciting and challenging to give anything but a sound "yes" response.

I wondered if I could find ample topics on which to write in the beginning. However, as the articles evolved I discovered that I possesed a wealth of information. I realize that countless individuals along the way have made their contributions through their knowledge, guidance, love, and support. They must be acknowledged.

My first appreciation and tribute goes to Shinichi Suzuki for the beautiful gift he has given to the world, the Suzuki method. Without it, none of the rest would have been possible.

There are those from whom I gained my initial training to thank. They planted the seeds in me that grew and developed into flowers I had never before dreamed possible.

First is Lorraine Fink, my sons' violin teacher, who gave me my first knowledge. Through absorbing her teaching as a parent during years of lessons, her tremendous insights into the philosophy made a significant impact on me and deepened my understanding. For this reason, I consider her my greatest trainer.

Next came training with piano specialists of the method — Haruko Kataoka, Carole Bigler, and Valery Lloyd-Watts. Through them I learned the application of the philosophy to the piano. My teacher trainees, colleagues, and friends have been highly supportive and encouraging over the years. In particular I wish to thank my friends Ginny and Larry Christopherson, and Reginald Fink, my friend and publisher.

Last, I must include Mae, my very special aunt, for first instilling in me a love of music. I still remember the hot but wonderful summer nights when I was a tiny child that she sang me to sleep as we swung on the front porch of our North California home. Her love and support of my music over the years has meant a great deal.

To all the above as well as many unnamed, I extend my grateful appreciation. They are all an integral and important part of my results.

Mary Craig Powell

Chapter 1

Focus on Philosophy

"If love is deep, much can be accomplished." These words from Shinichi Suzuki, founder of the Suzuki method, provide powerful insight into the man, the philosophy, and the method.

The Suzuki method began with Dr. Suzuki's realization that a child displays phenomenal abilities when he learns to speak his native language (mother tongue) during his early years of life. Learning to speak a new language is difficult for an older student to accomplish, but every young child does this—and long before he learns to read. Suzuki felt that we must learn how to develop the amazing potential that every child possesses; furthermore, we must acknowledge the fact that ability, not only in music but in other fields as well, is not inherited. Man is born without talent and his environment controls what he becomes. Others had realized this before. Suzuki's genius lay in his ability to develop an educational method which grows logically from its underlying philosophy.

A summary of Suzuki's philosophy is as follows:
The Suzuki philosophy embraces the belief that all children have great potential and that their abilities can be developed best by making use of that learning process which is universally most natural to all children—the Mother Tongue approach. Therefore, the Suzuki method of musical instruction parallels virtually without modification the same course that the child experiences from infancy in the learning of his language skills.

Since Dr. Suzuki is a violinist, he applied the method first to the violin. We who teach Suzuki piano are grateful for the outstanding contributions of Mrs. Haruko Kataoka and Mrs. Shizuko Suzuki who worked with Dr. Suzuki in order to adapt the method to the study of piano.

The Suzuki method, also called Talent Education, is based upon certain fundamental ideas that must be mentioned in order to gain a comprehensive picture of it. They are as follows:

1. Early Beginning. It is believed that the ability of a child to learn by aural means is strongest from birth to age seven. Thus, a method which relies heavily on aural capability is best begun early in order to use it to its greatest advantage. It should be mentioned, however, that numerous children over seven have begun and successfully enjoyed the method also.

2. Emphasis on Listening. Listening is considered the most important part of the Suzuki method. Recordings and tapes of the literature the Suzuki students are to learn are played repeatedly in their homes. Through listening, the children absorb unconsciously the language of music just as they absorb the sounds of their mother tongue.

Additionally, keyboard instruction through a listening approach is stressed. Emphasis is placed upon teaching by demonstration; the child imitates what he hears and sees.

3. Reading. Good Suzuki teachers value the skill of reading music as much as traditional teachers. The difference is that reading music is not taught first in the Suzuki method, but delayed until the child's aural and basic keyboard skills are established. Just as the child enters first grade in school with a large vocabulary of speech but minimal reading skills, the Suzuki student's musical capabilities have developed in the same way. It is expected that the child's reading skills will catch up to his vocabulary in five to ten years. The Suzuki child's ability to read music will progress in a similar fashion.

4. Psychology. A non-judgmental psychology with great emphasis on positive reinforcement is stressed in the Suzuki method. Dr. Suzuki developed his method as a result of his love for children and a desire to create a more beautiful world for them. A method based on love and concern for the child must embody such a psychology.

5. One-Step-at-a Time. Mastery is accomplished by a one-step-at-a-time approach. Each step, no matter how small, is to be mastered before continuing to the next step.

6. Repertoire. Repertoire learned by the Suzuki student is continually maintained. Through repetition of pieces, old skills can be strengthened, new skills can be gained, and fluidity can be given to the playing.

7. Parental Involvement. Suzuki parents are an integral part of a Suzuki program. Their role is two-fold: 1) to attend the lessons in order to learn and model from the teacher; and 2) to provide the proper home environment. This includes supervising the practice and seeing that the listening is done.

8. Group Involvement. Although Suzuki students usually take private lessons, many Suzuki piano teachers encourage group involvement as well. These groups, which may meet once a week, or perhaps less frequently, especially help to provide motivation for the students. Although structured differently by individual teachers, most include an opportunity for the child to play a piece. Many teachers combine the performances with theory and musical enrichment of some type.

The principles discussed here must be understood by the Suzuki teacher and parent. For the teacher, serious training to learn the techniques of teaching the method is also required. As the leader, the teacher passes them on to the mother and child.

Instruction begins with a set of variations on *Twinkle, Twinkle Little Star*. Their importance cannot be overrated. They form the basis for the development of the child's technique. The method unfolds from this careful beginning.

The Suzuki method is praised for its success in developing the child to his fullest potential and for producing superior playing abilities. Dr. Suzuki's emphasis, however, has been and remains on using the method primarily to develop human beings who will make a better world filled with peace rather than war. It is a message of love.

Chapter 2

Focus on Parents

The Confident Parent

Recently I taught at a workshop where a young Suzuki piano teacher was doing an excellent job with her students. At a question-answer session with the parents, a mother of one of her students expressed to me that she felt she could do so little in terms of effective practice at home. She knew nothing about music, she said, and really wondered if she could make it work. She was a very intelligent woman—a medical doctor—but she did not feel certain that she could help her two children who were studying with this fine teacher.

I was struck by the fact that even the very best of teachers need to be more acutely aware of their students' parents in order to give them confidence. After all, they (the parents) work with the children six or seven times to our one each week. We need them to be effective!

As I travel and talk with teachers, this point is further confirmed by the fact that the questions often foremost in their minds are those relating to working efficiently with parents. I have struggled with the same problems myself for years. As a result, I would like to share some of my efforts that have proved meaningful in preparing, training, and helping my own Suzuki parents.

Lay the Ground Work for Success in the Beginning

In order to lay the groundwork for beginning parents, I like to begin with a parent meeting. I make certain that I cover the following points in the course of the meeting:

1. Basic philosophy

2. Book to read (mine read *Nurtured by Love* and/or *Ability Development from Age Zero*)

3. The role of the parent in a Suzuki program in the lesson and at home.

Under the role of the parent in the lesson I discuss:

• **Attendance**—the need to attend all weekly lessons.

• **Note-Taking**—I ask for a specific notebook to be purchased to avoid loose pieces of paper for notes that are easily lost. I also strongly recommend a tape recorder at the lesson.

• **Younger Siblings**—I ask that a sitter be arranged for the younger siblings. The parent is then free to direct his undivided attention to the lesson.

• **Discipline**—Parents are asked to let me handle any necessary discipline in the lesson.

• **Seating**—The parent is asked to sit in the special chair provided for him so that he can see the lesson to his best advantage.

• **Modeling**—The parent is to use the lesson as a means of learning to model after the teacher in the home practice. I assure him that I will do all possible in the lessons to help facilitate this.

Under the role of the parent at home, we discuss the two areas of responsibility they hold:

• **Listening**—We discuss the importance of listening in a Suzuki program. I give them concrete suggestions. These include: **a.** Length of daily listening—I ask for an hour a day as a mandatory amount in the beginning. **b.** Specific literature to hear—This includes a request to tape each working piece continuously 10 to 50 times. Secondly, I ask that the current piece and the ones to follow soon after are given the majority of the listening time. **c.** Suggested times to listen—this includes meals, bedtime, quiet play time, and time in the car.

• **Practicing**—There are so many points that can be made about practice that it could be easy to overwhelm. Here are some I choose to highlight: **a.** Make practice a daily routine **b.** Encourage several short practices a day in the beginning rather than one long session. **c.** Work on one point at a time. (It is up to the teacher to show how to implement this.) d. Praise—We want parents to know that we endorse a positive relationship with the child in the Suzuki method and we want them to strive to do so at home also.

(Note: If you only have one or two beginning parents, or if you prefer anyway, this information can be presented to the parent at the first lesson. The main point is to be certain they are given these facts in the beginning.)

Let the Parent Take the First Lesson

I always ask a new parent to provide a sitter for her child for the first lesson (or possibly two) and give the lesson to the parent alone. During this session I introduce *Twinkle A* techniques. These two steps are covered:

1. I work with the parent's hand at the piano as I would with the child's and thus let her experience Twinkle A techniques.

2. I guide the parent in working with my hand to provide experience for working with the child later at home. By the time she has worked with me for awhile, she feels substantially more confident about helping her child once his lessons are begun. Our dialogue might run as follows:

"You are beginning to get a good tone. Now can you increase the speed? We always begin right up to tempo." After the parent tries again I add, "That was a better tempo that time. Now I like the tone, the tempo, and the confidence I am feeling from you as you hold my hand and arm to play. You will be able to give Johnny a positive beginning with these kinds of skills developing."

(**Note:** Be sure the parent understands that she is to wait until the child begins the following week before starting to begin this work at home. The teacher is the one who should introduce these techniques to the child.)

In addition to *Twinkle* work, use this time to ask and take notes of the parent's previous musical background. If she knows nothing or very little about music, assure her that you plan to guide her in every way possible. Begin by teaching her the alphabet names of the notes on the keyboard. Later you can show her the names of the lines and spaces on the music staff. Continue to remain aware of her degree of knowledge as you progress through the books so you can guide her as needed. Welcome her questions as well.

Let the Parent Actively Participate in the Lessons in the Beginning

There are several ways of involving the parent with the lessons in the beginning which work well. One is to have her work with the child's hand and techniques as she did with the teacher's in the first lesson. She can watch the teacher work first, and then follow her example. When she practices with the child at home after these experiences, she should feel prepared. We have set the stage for success.

A suggestion is to put the parent at the piano to play along with the child and teacher for part of the lesson. Even if there is only one piano in the studio, she can sit at the bass end, the child in the middle, and teacher at the treble. It can work beautifully. Consider having each person take a turn playing a phrase of *Twinkle*.

A third suggestion is to give the child (who might be becoming restless anyway) a break from the piano bench and allow the parent to take a turn playing. At this time new *Twinkle* techniques might be presented. With each new *Twinkle* the parent will be more effective at home if she can play it herself. There is no need to make her feel on the spot about her performance; just stress the need for her to be able to play the basics in order to best understand them and consequently help her child at home. As for the child, it will be fun to have mother or dad play.

When the child knows each *Twinkle* well, consider teaching the parent Alberti I, IV, and V chords to accompany the child's right hand. This provides the pleasure of ensemble, additional strength for the child by playing one part against the other, and gives the parent basic left hand skills that will aid him tremendously through Book 1.

As my students continue through Book 1, I do not insist that the parents play additionally in the lessons unless they request it. However, I encourage all my parents to be able to play each hand alone at least in the privacy of their own home. While not having to deal with the coordination of two hands (if they are not pianists) they are at least understanding each hand and many of the problems of each piece. After the child knows each right hand piece thoroughly I ask that the parent play the left hand part with him as a part of his practice. This serves as an intermediate step between playing hands alone and together for the child.

Giving Guidance Toward the Home Practicing and Listening

"How is the listening going?" I often ask. "Are you managing to find an hour a day for it?" Such questions show that you care and also help to keep the parents "on their toes." Similar questions can be asked regarding the practice. In addition, concrete suggestions can and should be given about the practice on a weekly basis. Games and charts can be suggested. Be specific in your assignments. Offer help toward planning the practice sessions. Take time to summarize the assignment at the conclusion of the lesson.

Help the Parents Learn to Listen

Many intelligent parents have expressed to me their concern that they can teach the notes and fingerings, but they cannot tell if the results are musical. We need them to be able to hear good tone versus bad tone, good rhythm versus bad, *etc.* How can we provide them more confidence and break through this difficult barrier?

My first suggestion is to make certain the parent is listening at home as well as the child. Often I discover that the child is going to bed with the tape playing in his room (which is wonderful), but the parent is not hearing enough to build his own confidence in knowing the pieces he has to teach. Even the musician parent can improve his ear and insights into the music through increased listening.

I have been able to instill confidence and generate effectiveness in the parents by involving them in the listening activities in the lesson. For example, I often play a musical passage two ways in order to have them choose which way is better. Ask the child AND parent what they think. This type of involvement will foster alertness in the lesson as well as increase the parent's confidence in judging good musical results.

A second example of this type of involvement is one of my students' favorite lesson activities. I ask the parent to close her eyes and listen to the child and me play an identical passage (usually a short phrase or passage from a piece that we are endeavoring to improve). The goal is for the two players to sound so alike that they cannot be distinguished. After mother has listened to us, I ask such questions as "Was the tempo of the two players the same?" or "What about the tone?" The parent might answer that both players sounded good but she did notice that the fourth finger note of the second player (the child) sounded a little weaker than the first player's.

This technique serves a two-fold purpose. First, I have never seen a child yet who did not double his concentration and efforts in order to make the decision difficult for the parent. Consequently, I sometimes get results from the child that simply did not come before such a challenge. As for the parents, there are so many benefits it is difficult to list them all. For our purposes of the moment, the most important is that they are learning to listen and become discerning of musical results to a fine degree. Any parent who can hear one finger in a passage in which the tone differs slightly is REALLY learning to listen!

Be Sensitive to Your Parents

Parents come in all varieties and styles. Their responses can be as different as the types of people they are. Some seem relaxed, some scared and nervous, some efficient, some pressuring, some negative, and others positive. Not only do we need to give attention to them in terms of teaching the musical needs, but we need to nurture them as we see their individual needs. All of them need encouragement. Certainly they all have times when the practicing might not be going well. Seldom does any home escape periods of personal problems or sickness. We need as teachers to recognize their feelings and needs, just as we do the child's. Some extra reassurance and gentleness on our part might be all they need to help them move on. Each is an important individual and must be treated as such. Include their name in the praise. "Susie, you and Mother (or Dad) did a super job with your practice this week." Share your smile of pleasure at the time with *both* of them.

A Word of Appreciation

I, for one, have been both a Suzuki parent as well as a teacher. I KNOW that the parent has the greatest challenge in a Suzuki program. My heartfelt appreciation goes to those committed parents who care enough to give their children a beautiful Suzuki experience. May we all continue to help, nurture, and appreciate them in every way possible!

Parent-Teacher Communication

A recent visitor from England observed a number of Suzuki teachers and their programs around the United States. Her concluding comment noted that she had seen marvelous creativity among Suzuki teachers as they worked with their students, but she felt that the communication between the teachers and parents during lessons was weak. It is certainly a thought-provoking statement. Perhaps we need to think about what we can do to improve ourselves in this area.

There are some simple techniques that we as teachers can use to improve our communication with the parents. These do not necessarily involve extra talking or extra lesson time, but are simple aids toward giving directions more effectively. In fact, a number of them save time almost immediately, and all will have long-term benefits. Some are as follows:

Be Specific in All Assignments

We, as teachers, often mistakenly assume that mother understands exactly how to practice with the child when she arrives home. If we have spent extra time on a troublesome spot in the lesson, we feel she will definitely work on it. The less we assume, and the more specific we are in assigning, the better results we achieve. When we give specific directions, mothers get bright eyes because they are confident of what to do when they arrive home. Also, the child is usually far more willing to work for the teacher's special requests than for mother's. For example, a child in Book 1 who is just learning to play with hands together on a piece might receive an assignment such as this:

1. Practice right hand five times daily.

2. Practice left hand five times daily.

3. Duet three of those times with mother (meaning that mother plays right hand while the child plays left, then vice-versa.)

4. Then try playing hands-together five times.

Many more specifics can accompany these directions. On the five times alone for right hand the child might focus on a beautiful legato or beautiful tone. On the left hand alone he might focus on keeping it soft so that it can balance later with the right hand. Whatever the need, be sure to state it to avoid meaningless repetitions at home that reinforce bad habits rather than good.

If we have worked on special measures or parts, we need to be very specific in seeing that mother and child understand exactly how to practice those passages. Suggest special games, charts, or creative ideas that can be used that week toward achieving the desired goals. A teacher who uses the metronome can give specific assignments for desired tempi to be practiced, whether they be slow, medium, fast, or a combination of all.

Number the Measures

Ask that all your parents make a practice of numbering measures in each piece being studied. This eliminates having to take the time to tediously count and say "The passage we are discussing, mother, begins on the fourth line, seventh measure." Instead, we can simply state the measure number that needs citing.

Encourage Good Note-Taking at the Lesson

It is hoped that most teachers have asked the parent to take good notes and perhaps bring a tape recorder before ever beginning lessons with the child. However, if the parent becomes lax about this, a statement such as "We are getting into so many more details with the music than we used to that I think you would find it helpful to write some of them down," might help. Encourage the tape recorder, for there can be details missed in writing, or there can be some confusion upon arriving home over an assignment that the tape recorder can clear by using it to review the lesson.

Use Check Marks in the Margins and Measures

As the teacher follows the score in the lesson and sees points she wants to remember to discuss when the child's performance is concluded, a check (or some other appropriate mark) in the margin, as well as in the measure needing attention, not only helps her to avoid overlooking any notes or sections that need her comments and help, but also helps mother find them later. A comment such as, "I checked the margins and measures that need extra attention to help you find them when you get home," can be stated. Even mothers who do not take notes as effectively as we would like can find the checks at home.

Discuss Practice

The amount of practice time a child needs, especially in the early stages, is constantly changing and increasing. Many parents have no idea of the approximate time they should be practicing with their child. Without some input from the teacher, they may never know, and chances are they may not plan on enough. Suggestions such as "Practice several short times a day in the beginning," or "Try to play some review pieces before school each day," are helpful. Parent meetings are excellent for discussing practice problems, but lessons are more appropriate for the teacher to discuss the amount of time she feels each child should be practicing.

Help the parent plan the practice sessions. Suggest approximate time that needs to be spent in each area, whether it be technique, reading, review, or current repertoire. Perhaps some days the reading can be done before the Suzuki pieces, then alternated on other days. Let mother know that consistency with these things is most important.

Star Measures Needing Attention

A sign of special meaning, such as a star, can be replaced by measures that need special repetition during the week. Stars can mean to both the child and to mother that a measure or passage needs extra attention.

Talk to Mother Through The Child

There is a danger of losing the child's interest if we direct too many statements to mother without involving the child; he can begin to feel restless and uninterested when not involved. Such statements as "I want mother to write these steps to follow as we work through them in your reading assignment," or "You and mother practice starting this piece five times each day, listening for a beautiful tone on the first note each time," give specific directions to mother, but are directed through the child.

Discuss Listening

We might ask "How is the listening going?" on a periodic basis. It is very difficult to impress parents with the importance of enough listening. The fact that we ask periodically tells them that we consider it an important part of their child's Suzuki education. If it seems that their answer implies that they are having difficulty in doing the prescribed listening, then ask them if you may help. Perhaps a new suggestion from the teacher will give them the spark they need to try to increase that listening.

Summarize Assignments

Some teachers write the assignment; others verbalize it. Regardless of which method is used, it is good to summarize for the child and parent's benefit. That way, anything that was not clear before can be settled. Priorities for the week's practice can be given as well.

Conclusion

It is easy to become so involved in teaching the child a creative lesson that we forget that part of our responsibility is to see that the parent is able to implement our techniques effectively at home. Our challenge is to be clever enough to maintain that creativity for which our English visitor praised us while we find skillful, time-saving ways to communicate our ideas to parents. It takes both to build the successful Suzuki program we would like.

Chapter 3

Focus on Home Practice

10 Points on Practice

Practice—a topic worthy of many books and articles on the subject! It is probably the most challenging aspect of the parent's role in the Suzuki program. It can often be the most frustrating. Points about practice need to be discussed often to help parents with this challenge. Here are some suggestions:

Be Consistent

Establish a habit of regular daily practice. Music is like math; it demands consistent work in order to develop skills—not two hours one day and none for the next two days. This regularity will not only improve the child's skills, but will develop a discipline in the child that will carry into other areas throughout his entire life.

Know How Much Practice Is Needed

Parents and teachers should discuss practice time frequently, for the amount of practice needed changes periodically, especially in the beginning stages. For example, the pre-school beginner often has no formal practice session, but sits down frequently for five to ten-minute intervals as a way of initiating him into the longer practice sessions to follow. The amount of time needed changes quite rapidly as the child progresses through Book I; soon it builds to thirty minutes, then forty-five minutes, then an hour, and so on. The parent really has no way of knowing what is needed unless there is some indication from his teacher.

Find the Proper Time To Practice

Find the time best suited to your family needs and schedule. Perhaps before school or after dinner would fit best, or perhaps you can divide the practice into two sessions a day. Whatever works for you with regard to time is best.

Make the Review Meaningful

1. Focus on "one-point"—The purpose of review sessions can be meaningless unless there is some purpose and goal in them. Children often rush through these pieces, setting wild tempos and possibly doing more harm than good. In Japan the students are taught "one-point" lessons where they are to concentrate on one specific goal for the week, such as tone quality, dynamics, balance, etc. Why not consider a "one-point" focus each week in your review, thus avoiding the meaningless playing that can so easily happen with even the best of students?

2. Control the review—Be sure to control the review so that all pieces are covered within a designated period of time. Pieces that are lost from lack of repetition are frustrating to regain.

Plan the Practice Session

Often parents can use some guidance along this line. The tendency is to spend too much time on the newest Suzuki piece. A suggested practice procedure could be:

1. Begin with some review—Something familiar loosens the child's hands and arms and establishes the sound in his ears of good results already achieved to be followed on newer pieces. Psychologically, it provides the advantage of gradually working toward the more difficult literature of the newest piece, so that the piece does not seem overwhelming when reached.

2. Do Technique Early in Practice—Any technique assigned, such as tonalization or scales, makes a logical early-practice step, also. This can serve the same purpose as a runner who does warm-ups before running.

3. Work on the Reading Assignment—Spend approximately one-third of your practice time here, once it is begun.

4. Practice the New Suzuki Material—Again, about one-third of the practice time can be spent here.

5. End with Review—Be sure to let some of this be the child's choice.

(**Note:** Consider alternating the order of steps three and four daily. This helps avoid being over-tired on the same pieces by the time the later portion of the practice is reached.)

Make Music Reading a Daily Habit

Parents often fail to understand that reading is a skill that must be done daily in order to develop. A few minutes spent each day are worth more than a few longer sessions a couple of times a week.

Set Goals for Motivation

Practice is much more interesting and motivating when there are goals. Many can be simple ones such as preparing pieces for weekly mini-recitals at home for dad or friends. Taping pieces to send to grandparents, other relatives, or friends as a present or surprise can be a delightful goal. Teachers can set goals outside the home for students through recitals, group lessons, and through participation in local and national music organizations which provide events for playing, such as festivals.

Plan Your Techniques for Practicing the Suzuki Material

1. Begin the Work on Special Passages or Sections—Many children tend to feel that once they have played through a piece they have finished practicing it. When the parent asks to go back and work on a special passage, they sometimes meet with resentment. Try the opposite approach. Work on the special passages needing extra repetition first and then play the entire piece. There seems to be a psychological advantage to this.

2. Have the Teacher Suggest the Number of Repetitions on Each Piece or a Certain Passage Daily. Children will often do this more willingly at the teacher's request than at the parent's.

Recognize the Child's Need to Become Independent

As the child becomes older and more advanced, a time approaches when the parent needs to help the child become less dependent on her in practice. Some children want independence; others do not. However, the responsibility any parent has to their child is to wean him from total dependency at birth to complete independence as a mature and responsible adult. With the caring parent, this process is a gradual one. So it should be with helping the child become independent in his practice—a gradual process. Perhaps these suggestions will help.

1. Begin Independence with a Specific Reading Piece. Let the child begin to prepare one reading piece totally on his own each week. The teacher might possibly choose a less difficult piece for this purpose. Basic reading skills need to be established before this is done, however.

2. Begin Independent Practice Gradually. Instead of working with the entire reading assignment daily with the child, try helping him early and late in the week; let the child practice it on his own in the middle of the week.

3. Alternate Days for Independent Work. Begin alternating days for hearing the review and the technique. This way the child can play his review independently one day and scales and/or other techniques the next day. The parent can be within hearing range as the child works, but not sitting beside him.

4. Continue to Supervise New Suzuki Piece. Ease away from the new Suzuki piece last. The child needs the parent's help in this area more than any other.

5. Continue to Show Interest After Complete Independence Is Established. Continue to show interest and support even though you are not actively involved in the practice when this point is reached. Many children enjoy having their parents in the room as they practice, even though the parents might be reading the paper or mending socks. Many parents continue to attend the child's lesson in order to show their continued support. Remember that weaning away from the child's practice does not mean weaning away from interest. This entire process is a sensitive one and needs to be handled carefully.

Make Practice Fun, Loving and Positive

Dr. Suzuki once said that "Children have very wonderful minds—they are just short." Dr. Haim Ginott, a renowned child psychologist and author, said that "The best way to a child's mind is through his heart." Reaching those wonderful minds through their hearts can be achieved to a large extent through creative ideas and games that keep the practice fun and positive, with some extra hugs and praise mixed in. Make a point to find every game and creative idea possible. Many articles contain these ideas; teachers and Suzuki institutes provide constant new suggestions on the subject.

In conclusion, remember that whatever ideas you use, practice is a very special time you and your child have together. You will both remember it the rest of your life. *How* you remember it is so important! Let us hope it will be thought of as a time when a positive and warm relationship was established between the two of you—one that was "nurtured by love."

Ten Thousand Times!

Repeat, repeat, repeat—such basic words these are to our Suzuki tenets. "Ten thousand times" are the words used by Dr. Suzuki. He states that repetition develops motor skills. It develops persistence in the child who is learning a skill, and it develops self-esteem in the child who has achieved a skill.

The challenge for the teacher and parent is to keep the repetition interesting. We must be creative enough to maintain the child's interest through the ten thousand times.

There are a number of simple aids we can utilize. I would like to share with my readers some that have worked well and have become favorites with my students.

Assignment Sheets

Weekly assignment sheets prepared for the child that include specific assignments for repetition help provide motivation and structure for the home practice.

"Look at my assignment sheet, Mrs. Powell," Sarah says with a sparkle in her eyes. "The smiling faces are for my good work and the so-so faces are for just all right. Mother and I fill them in after every piece and repetition."

"That's neat, Sarah," I reply. "What are the stars for?"

"Oh, those are for the *extra* special good times. Look, I got five of those this week!" Sarah adds happily.

Special Charts

Sometimes the parents make a special chart for just one piece or passage, marking daily the number of repetitions done. For example, when my students begin Book 2, I like the first 16 measures of *Ecossaise* to be played 20 times a day. I always suggest that the students mark the repetitions on a chart and show it to me at the next lesson. They always return with a sense of pride and triumph as they show me their chart.

Stars and Stickers

Stars and stickers can be used in numerous ways. A successful way some of my Suzuki parents have used them has been to purchase a book of blank pages on which they write the title of each piece their child knows on a separate page. As the child repeats the piece or parts of it to his satisfaction, he is allowed to add a sticker to the page with the title of that particular piece. The more the repetitions, the more colorful and wonderful each page becomes!

Verbal Statements

There are numerous verbal statements to make repetitions more colorful. My students enjoy some of these suggestions from me:
"David, close your eyes and play that passage."

"Look at the ceiling and play it."

"Now look at Mother and play."

"Can you hold your left hand in the air while the right hand plays this passage?—Behind your back?—To your side?—Surely you couldn't stick out your tongue and hold your arm in the air at the same time. Fantastic! You did it."

In another lesson the dialogue might run:
"David, move your hand down an octave and play this passage. Sounds like Grandad's voice, doesn't it! Listen to the friendly dragon in the dungeon (octave lower)—If you think he sounds funny, just listen to the dragon's grandad (lowest octave) when he plays!"

At another time I pretend to play doctor and prescribe five to ten vitamin pills a day on a particular passage to make it as healthy as the rest.

Use of Games

Most children love games and learn a great deal by playing them. Games to provide repetition are excellent. Here are some suggestions:

Scramble—The scramble card game provides a wonderful opportunity for repetition. In this game, as presented by Bigler and Watts in *Studying Suzuki Piano: More Than Music*, playing cards represent the parts or phrases of the music. The aces are part 1, the 2's are part 2, *etc.* To play, the parent or teacher holds the cards in her hands so the child cannot see the numbers; then, he draws and plays the part he has received. If a child needs extra repetition on a particular part, Mother can "stack the deck" with that part.

"Simon Says"—A child who is not wanting to repeat for some reason is often thrilled to do so because "Simon says" to play that part 10 times!

Counting Games—Numerous objects can be used in these games. A stack of pennies moved one by one from one pile to another will keep many a child repeating happily to achieve the good results to make the moves. Erasers of various shapes are popular counting items in my studio. These are found often in toy stores, drug stores, and teachers' aids stores. To use them, line them up on one side of the piano and move them to the other side with the achievement of each goal. Erasers are preferable to pennies because pennies often fall in the cracks between the piano keys and also can scratch the piano. Neither of these problems exists with erasers.

New Materials Offer Variety

New materials on the Suzuki market in the last few years are making the challenge of finding new ideas for repetition easier for parents and teachers. Two books now available that contain excellent ideas are *I Love to Practice* by Patricia J. Steiner and Yvonne B. Halls and *Mommy, Can We Practice Now* by Marie C. Parkinson. The *Perfectly Silly Perfect Game* by Michiko Yurko offers hours of pleasure for the young student. With this kind of pleasure in the practice, the child is hardly aware he is repeating and repeating.

Advanced Level of Repetition

Difficult passage work in the upper volumes needs to have countless ways provided for repetition. Commonly used among pianists of advanced levels are varying combinations of rhythms on these passages. For example, with  passage work in 3/4 time, there are three rhythms to which it can be changed. They are:

In triplet passage work the rhythms are changed to duple:

In addition to the above, a wonderful practice technique for a passage is to stress the offbeats. For example, in a passage of four 16th notes, the second and fourth notes are accented. This is a terrific exercise for strengthening fingers that are not normally stressed.

An easier but still valuable exercise for passage work is to change even notes into dotted rhythms. Even young students at the Book 3 level can handle this exercise.

Use of Metronome

A teacher can gain valuable repetitions by giving specific metronome speeds with each week's practice assignment on a piece. Slow, medium, and fast repetitions can be listed. Slow metronome speeds can provide the discipline for slow practice that is difficult to accomplish on one's own. Gradual movement to faster levels can bring about the speed needed coupled with real control in playing a passage. Moving from slow to fast with the metronome can give a student a fine sense of accomplishment.

Conclusion

Each child is different. Games and colorful ideas can over-excite some children. For others they are not needed. Most children respond well to them and for those who do, these ideas are wonderful as long as the teacher and parent keep in mind that the end result is the achievement of new skills or improved skills rather than playing games for the sake of merely providing amusement, entertainment, and fun. Learning IS fun! These suggestions are to help contribute to an atmosphere that is positive, enjoyable, relaxed, and conducive to good learning.

Enjoy repetition!

Chapter 4

Focus on Listening

Learning to Listen

"Most students hear, but they do not listen. The finest students are those who have learned to listen." Josef Lhevinne: **Basic Principles of Pianoforte Playing.**

Much has been written and spoken about the importance of listening in the Suzuki philosophy. Every knowledgeable Suzuki teacher and parent is aware that a large amount of daily listening to the Suzuki recordings and tapes is essential. This type of listening is inherent to our method and must be done in order for the child to develop to the utmost of his potential.

But there is another aspect of listening equally as important: that of teaching the child to listen to himself as he plays. Although I have many students with highly developed ears, I am constantly aware that they are not using them to their fullest potential as they play. This problem can develop especially easily with pianists because they do not have to listen in order to play in tune as most instrumentalists do.

I am convinced of two facts regarding listening to oneself. First, it is basic to fine playing. Walter Gieseking, one of the foremost pianists of the century, underscores throughout his book, *Piano Technique*, that emphasis on listening to oneself and proper understanding are the bases of correct technique for the piano. Second, I believe that there is no greater method for developing this ability in the student than the Suzuki method.

How can we utilize this method to its fullest? I would like to share with you the techniques and ideas that work best for me.

Teaching Through Demonstration and Imitation

This approach is basic to our philosophy. However, many traditionally-oriented teachers have been fearful of this type of teaching for years. I was never afraid that talking with my own children would prevent them from being able to express themselves creatively when they became adults. Neither am I afraid to play and demonstrate for my students. Through this I am giving them the musical discipline in which they can grow. Within these boundaries will flow creativity as well.

Imitation follows the demonstration. It is an "I play, you play" approach with as little verbalizing as possible. I pursue it over and over through all six volumes and beyond.

In my opinion, imitation is the finest way to approach almost every musical and technical problem because it undergirds a basic principle of learning—the principle of learning through discovery. Something discovered (in this case through imitation) is something learned well—far better than if the child is simply told what to do (verbalization). Also, it is the simplest, quickest, and most efficient way to elicit beautiful results.

The demonstration and imitation process is the key to success in developing the student's ability to learn to listen to himself. Coupled with this are other techniques to further develop and heighten the listening ability.

Giving Choices

Giving choices through demonstration can help the student and parent develop taste and musical discrimination. For example, Joel was playing *Twinkle A* with a harsh tone during his lesson. I asked him to listen as I played and help decide if my tone sounded happy (good) or angry (bad). He quickly discerned the difference in the sounds, as did his mother.

"You hear that so well, Joel," I exclaimed. "Now *you* play and let Mother and me decide about your tone." A new awareness of good sound had been created in Joel from his choice-making and he improved his tone to the happy one we were seeking almost immediately.

In addition, I never had to tell him that his initial tone was dreadful; I simply helped him to improve it by making use of demonstration, choice-making, and imitation. It is a beautiful process. Not only does it bring about change quickly, but it can be handled in a positive manner, thus leaving the child feeling good about himself and his new results.

Choice-making through demonstration can be used in endless ways. Before a child goes home to begin a new piece, a quick decision about which of two ways the piece might sound best can prepare the parent and child for success by clarifying their musical goals for it.

For example, *Clair de Lune* is Becky's new working piece. I give a choice to her and Mother by asking, "Which sounds more like your tape—for me to play it this way (I play with very detached repeated notes on the three opening notes) or in another way (with legato repeated notes)?" Becky and Mother quickly agree that the second way sound like their tape. We then discuss how we will make that happen. Becky is now sensitized to what she must listen for and produce as she learns the new piece.

Asking Direct Questions

Other types of questioning based on listening can lead to making fine musical decisions. For example, Corey is learning the left hand of *Happy Farmer.* He plays the first note (the upbeat) with a strong accent and the second note (the downbeat) with less emphasis. I play the first four notes of the piece for him, stressing the downbeat.

"Which note did I make the most special, Corey?" I ask. Corey points to the F, the downbeat note. "Good for you for hearing that," I respond, "I like it that way. It makes it begin as though the farmer is saying 'I love to sing'. Now you try it."

When Corey tries and plays the F heavily but unattractively, I say, "Listen to my farmer, Corey, and tell me which way you like best. Which way makes him sound as if he really loves to sing?" I play a first example which duplicates Corey's first attempt, and a second with a beautiful, warm, full tone on the downbeat.

Corey smiles and responds that he likes the second example. We agree the first way sounds as if the farmer hates to sing. Then I have him play while Mother and I listen to hear if his farmer loves or hates to sing. Corey listens to himself, also—with real discrimination.

Following Through

"You did so well, Corey, that I want to hear you play some more beautiful examples for me," I state. "We'll all take turns deciding if we like them." Corey plays and I decide; then Mother; and then Corey himself. By this time I am certain that he and Mother hear and know what is a beautiful sound and feel confident to do the same at home without me. "Let's have you play this five beautiful times a day at home this week. Next lesson I am looking forward to hearing your farmer again." I also make a reminder in my notebook to follow up on this point at Corey's next lesson.

Close Your Eyes

Jenny is learning to play *Twinkle D.* A few of her repeated notes are unequal in length because they are not held long enough. "Jenny," I say, "I want you to close your eyes and listen to me play *Twinkle D.* If you hear any notes that bother you—such as any that sound as if they have the hiccups, please raise your hand." This is a familiar and favorite game for this young pre-Twinkler and she quickly closes her eyes. I begin playing with a few intentional hiccups played intermittently between the musical ones. Jenny's hand pops up for every one of my mistakes.

"You hear those so well!" I exclaim. "Let's have you play while I close my eyes. I'll raise my hand if I hear any notes that bother me. Try to keep me from raising my hand." Jenny plays with tremendously improved discrimination in listening to herself and soon I complain, "Jenny, this is no fun. I never get to raise my hand for you!"

Happy Faces

A pleasant and highly effective way to help a child listen to himself and make musical decisions is through the use of happy faces. This idea works well for the child and mother to use at home in their daily practice. Round faces can be drawn on a blank piece of paper before the child plays a designated piece or passage. These faces can look three ways when filled in:

Upon completion of the piece, the child and mother decide how the face should be completed from the three choices. It is amazing how honest they are and how much this simple idea encourages them to listen to themselves.

Gieseking writes that listening to oneself is one of the most important factors of the whole music study. The Suzuki method gives us the tools to develop listening to a high degree in our students.

Listening Games to Sharpen Musical Concepts

The Legato Game

A concept introduced through the *Twinkle Variations* is legato. It is heard first through tonalization and the *Twinkle* theme. Dr. Suzuki has been quoted as saying to "hear first" when we learn; in striving to approach that goal, I have devised a listening game to strengthen the legato concept which I have simply named the "legato game." I have introduced it to my young students as they are showing a readiness to begin tonalization and the *Twinkle* theme. I would like to share it for it has been a successful teaching tool. A dialogue would run as follows:

Four-year-old Blake is having his piano lesson. "Blake," I say during the course of his lesson, "I want you to get off the piano bench and go sit beside Mother. In fact, I want you and Mother to join hands, close your eyes, and listen very carefully." Blake and Mother do as requested while I play up and down a five-finger major pattern in a very legato manner on the piano. I am careful not to define legato; we simply listen to it.

"Now, Blake and Mother, I am going to play something for you which is not legato. I want you to raise your joined hands when you hear something very different from the legato you just heard." This time I play the same five-finger pattern but insert a huge "hiccup" on one of the notes. Blake and Mother's hands immediately shoot up and they have a pleased expression on their faces.

"Good, both of you. That was good listening. Let's do some more." We then continue and they raise their hands for a few more very obvious breaks in the legato line. Holding hands with Mother has given Blake more confidence in making the decision to raise his hand for this first introduction to the game.

"You are doing so well that I think I must make it more difficult for you." This time the legato break I play is much less obvious. Blake is not as certain but looks as if he thinks he hears something different. I help by stating that if he is thinking he should raise his hand, he is correct. I continue the game with a mixture of easy, obvious breaks in the legato line and some more subtle, challenging ones. This way Blake and others like him can enjoy success on part of the game and improve at hearing the more sophisticated breaks at the same time.

"I want you and Mother to play this game at home this week." Blake nods happily, for he looks forward to practice of this nature. Since I have involved Mother in the game, I know that she, too, can hear legato. I make certain that she can also play legato by giving her a moment at the piano. Mother seems to appreciate this, for she now feels confident that she can go home and play the game with Blake successfully.

30

The next week Blake interrupts before we are very far into our lesson with "I want to play the legato game!" We play it and I discover that he and Mother are raising their hands with confidence even on the slightest breaks that I add to the legato line. Blake and Mother are no longer holding hands to support one another's decision either. I know from these results that the groundwork is well laid for playing a beautiful legato on the piano, for Blake can hear it now.

What a very beautiful and successful way it is to teach through this Suzuki philosophy—first we hear and then we learn. It makes learning easy!

Follow the Leader

An imitative game that has proven extremely valuable to me in my teaching is one I call "Follow the Leader." It is known to many as "Copycat" and is not innovative with me by any means. I have learned to use it many ways, however, and would like to share with you some of the values I have found in it.

I introduce "Follow the Leader" early—while the student is learning right hand on the *Twinkles*. At that point, my purpose is to aid melodic ear development. The child places his right hand on a five-finger pattern over C and I place mine in the same position an octave higher. In the beginning weeks the child is always allowed to watch my hand as well as listen in order to copy my patterns. Using the familiar rhythm of *Twinkle A*, I begin by very simply playing it with first finger, and the child returns with the same answer. Next I use two eighth notes ("hot dogs") on C. This is followed by eighth notes first on C and then on D. I am careful to use such simple patterns in the beginning to help the child be successful in returning his answer—thus he will feel good about the game and want to do more.

In the weeks that follow I give increasingly harder patterns in the lesson which the parent copies so he or she can do them at home daily. The parents are given finger numbers to use, but the child is to learn the patterns only by listening and watching—no finger numbers for him.

Steps are used first and skips are added later. A logical sequence of usable patterns for the beginning stages is as follows: (For convenience, I shall use finger numbers.)

11111 —	123455 —
1122 —	543211 —
112233 —	1133 —

As the child becomes increasingly confident in his skills, I have him close his eyes as I give the patterns; he then opens them to play. The teacher must be careful to begin the first few patterns on C, the tonic note, to establish the tonality in his ear. With the use of this game, coupled with the development coming from listening to the recording or tape, Suzuki students can "outshine" most college freshman music theory students in melodic dictation abilities within a short period of time.

The game need not be limited to melodic dictation, however. The teacher can use it as a tool to sharpen the child's awareness of many musical concepts. For example, a pattern can be played *forte,* then *piano.* Others can be done with a *crescendo* or *diminuendo,* with *staccato, legato* or accented touch, and with various tempi. Even the slightest of nuances and subtleties can be played for the child to answer by listening. Tricky passages to new pieces can be previewed. Some of the patterns become such finger twisters that they aid in strengthening dexterity and independence of the fingers. The challenge is to achieve all results through listening—except for a few words of praise, not a word need be exchanged between teacher and child.

I begin every child's lesson with this game for as long as he is in Book 1 and often pursue it with increased challenges in Book 2 as well. The benefits of beginning this way have been two-fold: the children enjoy the game; thus, it gives us a positive beginning. It also means that I have gained their concentration and have focused their ears on learning by listening from the very first moment we are together.

Chapter 5

Focus on Psychology

Points on Psychology for the Suzuki Teacher

Our Suzuki philosophy endorses a positive and non-judgmental psychology. Much is written, said, and stressed about it.

If I could return to school and select a second discipline to facilitate my teaching, it would be the field of child psychology. For years I have read books on the subject in order to enrich my approach toward my students. I do not pretend to be a psychologist in writing this article. However, I would like to share with you some of the things I have learned that have greatly improved working relationships with my students.

Give Choices Within Boundaries

Children need and like to be able to make choices. These are possible to give in lessons, provided we set the boundaries. A question given without boundaries can potentially bring difficult responses. For example, "What would you like to do next?" might evoke a response such as, "I would like to climb on your piano."

The same question with boundaries established such as, "What would you like to play next, *Lightly Row* or *Go Tell Aunt Rhody?*" is excellent. In this way, the child has had limitations set but feels a degree of flexibility within them. Children feel more secure within boundaries in all areas of their lives.

Praise and Criticize the Act

In Haim Ginott's book *Between Parent and Child*, he discusses the fact that praise and criticism must deal only with the child's efforts and accomplishments and not with his character and personality.

For example, when a child has played a piece beautifully, helpful praise from the teacher should be "Your performance was beautiful" (praise of the act) rather than "You are wonderful" (praise of the child). He explains that praise of the child's character and personality can make him feel guilty; he may have many thoughts about himself that cause him to feel far less than wonderful. Thus, our unhelpful praise can potentially impose guilt upon him.

The same is true of criticism. For a teacher or mother to tell a child "You are terrible" because a piece is played poorly is assaulting his character. Instead, find the source of the problem and deal directly with it. For example, if the problem has been with poor fingering, then a better approach would be to say, "I want to talk to your fingers for a moment."

State Your Boundaries in Matters of Discipline

When needed, state your disciplinary boundaries firmly and totally with the child. For example:
"I am the only one to touch the metronome in piano lessons. Then if it should break, I will be the one to have to pay for a new one."
or
"I have an important rule in piano lessons. It is that I want you to play the piano only when I ask you. When I am talking to Mother, it is about you and we need to be able to hear."

Understanding can accompany such statements. A concluding statement might be, "I know it will be a difficult rule to follow, but I want you to try."

Permit Leeway

Some leeway within our boundaries is often needed. Our little ones often need leeway granted since they are experiencing some of their first discipline outside of the home environment with us.

Most especially, leeway must be given if the child is extra tired or recovering from sickness. For example, the teacher might state, "You're tired today, Johnny. I have days when I feel that way, too. It's tough to take a lesson when you're feeling tired. We'll try this piece another day."

Express Your Own Feelings

It is important for children to know we have feelings and that there are healthy, respectable ways to vent them. However, our feelings for the child must be separated from feelings about the act. After an unbelievably trying lesson with Johnny, I stated, "I feel unhappy and frustrated today when I try to work with you and cannot. I always like you, Johnny, (feelings for the child) but I do not like to have such a difficult time working with you." (feelings about the act).

After such a strong statement, be sure to remember another time to state as strongly the opposite reaction. "Your lesson today made me feel so happy, Johnny. It was not only beautifully prepared, but it was such a pleasure to work with you!"

Allow the Freedom to Fail

Most children are concerned about making mistakes and failing at their efforts. They fear they will not meet with adult approval if they are not perfect. I am convinced that some children misbehave in their lessons rather than try to learn because it is better in their minds to misbehave than to fail when they try. Suggestions such as follow can help when one senses such feelings in the child:

Play a passage and make a few mistakes intentionally. Follow with a statement such as, "I hope you make a few mistakes, too. I certainly do sometimes."

Another possibility is, "I like people who make mistakes."

Role reversal in which you make mistakes for the child to correct is excellent. He consequently feels freer to make and then allow you to correct his mistakes.

I often demonstrate a passage a good and a bad way for a child and ask him which way he prefers. If I notice any reticence on his part to state his opinion I add, "It will be all right if we have two different opinions."

Always Be Honest

Always be honest with the child. For example, if the child performs poorly and we try to smooth over it and say we thought it was wonderful, we have been dishonest. Children know this and they lose a certain amount of trust and respect for a teacher who is dishonest. Instead, we can express our feelings in this manner:

"I know we both feel disappointed with your performance because we know how much better you can play. It's sad, but those performances happen to everybody at one time or another, even to me. I feel so proud of you for going ahead and finishing it, even though it was rough. That took a lot of courage and determination!"

Accentuate the Positive

Fill the lesson with "I likes" and save the negatives for the more forceful impact. The "I likes" implant confidence and train far better than the negatives. Even the areas needing improvement can often be expressed through positive approaches.

Negative: "You are terrible with your dynamics."
Positive: "You did such a nice job with dynamics in the last piece that I am certain we can do it here as well."

or

"When you are as good with your dynamics as you are with your fingering, this is going to be even better."

or

"This is showing such improvement I'm really feeling excited about it! Let's see what we can do to make it even more beautiful."

Negative: "Why don't you keep your feet still!"
Positive: "I'm going to wait until your feet are still."

For the child who has made a poor musical decision:
Negative: "You're wrong."
Positive: "I'd like to change your mind about it."

Address the Child by Name

Make a point to address the child frequently in the lesson by name. It generates a warmer, more personal feeling. Be sure to include eye contact along with it when possible.

Prepare for New Events

Psychologists recommend play-acting to prepare children for new events. Doing so before recitals or festivals can be fun.

Young children love to play-act for their "pretend audiences" of stuffed animals and dolls at home. Before recitals they enjoy the assignment of practicing walking to the stage, bowing, assuming fine posture and rest position before playing, getting into ready-set position, playing, resuming rest position, bowing, and returning to their seats from their pretend stage. After this kind of preparation the uncertainty is gone and they normally approach the stage with great confidence, even for their very first recital.

Years ago one of my young sons won a huge, pink, stuffed rabbit in a school drawing. Bugsy, as we named him, was about as round as he was tall with a warm, charming face—really quite an appealing fellow. I decided he would make an excellent judge for play-acting a festival that my students attend annually. The week prior to the festival Bugsy arrived at my studio. Each child went through the ritual of presenting him the music as we walked into the pretend festival room. After being seated, the child would then ask Bugsy if he could test the piano before beginning his piece. Every step was play-acted so that the stress of the unknown was relieved. It was such fun that the children began expecting Bugsy at their last lesson before the festival each year. Confident, secure performances emerged from children who knew what to expect.

36

A basic need of all mankind is to be loved from birth. Studies have shown that those who are not nurtured as infants are the individuals who most commonly develop psychopathic patterns of behavior in our society.

As teachers we have the opportunity to be sensitive to and nurture the child's need to be loved. Our nurturing might be our greatest gift to some children. Hugs and smiles are good. Also, the way we approach our students verbally throughout their lesson can show love or the lack of it. Thus, we see the reason to focus on psychology.

What more beautiful example can be found of that caring, nurturing adult than Dr. Suzuki? It was his deep love for children that precipitated the development of the Suzuki method. He has stated that "Where love is deep, much can be accomplished." In that sense, he is a great psychologist. We who love and adopt his philosophy must continually strive to emulate this great man.

"Fred"

In *Between Teacher and Child*, Haim Ginott has stated that "...to reach a child's mind, a teacher must first capture his heart." Psychologists have stated that the use of a puppet, stuffed animal, etc. as a means of dialogue with a child is good. It is in the spirit of both of these points that this story is revealed to my readers.

I would like to introduce you to my frog. His name is Fred and he is a

Mississippi Hop Frog. Fred is a bright green stuffed animal. Not only does he possess a most appealing face and body, but he is wonderfully soft, cuddly, and loveable.

Fred resides in my teaching studio and stations himself on my piano right where he can stare down attentively at all the hands that play Suzuki piano. He knows a great deal about teaching Suzuki piano. (I think this is due to the musical environment he has had since birth.) Because he has a better view of the positions of the hands and fingers than I, I depend on him for suggestions as to how to improve them. The poor fellow's eyes have become crossed from all that he has examined.

Fred is shy. Thus, he is unwilling to speak aloud during piano lessons. He whispers all his comments (and he has a lot of them) to me and I have to relay them to the students.

Fred has numerous facets to his personality. When asked if he likes something a student has done, he shows his approval by nodding his head with great enthusiasm and vigor. In fact, it even makes his eyes rattle.

He can be open about his dislikes, too. For example, he sometimes covers his eyes in horror or turns away so he doesn't have to look or listen. His openness surprises me at times. When he is highly excited about a fine accomplishment, he jumps in the air with joy. I never know what he is going to do next.

One of Fred's many merits is having the most relaxed arms imaginable. Indeed, he sets a wonderful example for little arms and hands needing to feel the same way at the piano. He demonstrates by flopping them freely.

Fred sometimes sits on an elevated shoulder of a student. He has a way while he sits there of making the child extremely conscious of this problem and improving it immediately. I am most appreciative of his help in this area.

What a fine assistant he is right from the beginning lessons. For example, as three-year-old Constance attempts playing "Mississippi Hop Frog" *Twinkle (Twinkle A)* with a somewhat harsh tone, Fred whispers in my ear, "She is making me sound like I'm an angry hop frog! Tell her to make me sound like a happy one instead."

Constance smiles as I tell her Fred's complaint and I proceed to demonstrate a happier tone that will please Fred. Constance tries after me. This time her tone sounds weak.

"Does that sound better, Fred?" I inquire. Fred decides to whisper again in my ear.

"Fred," I exclaim, "how could you be so hard to please! Constance, he says that now it sounds like he's a tired hop frog."

Constance giggles and proceeds to improve her tone until even Fred is pleased.

There is no doubt that Fred is a fussy frog. He is stubborn and wants skills accomplished just right. He is willing to have them done one step at a time, however. I am grateful he is that way, for otherwise he would be too overwhelming.

Fred gets away with his demands better than almost any human I have ever known. I believe it is because he never criticizes the children—just their problems. (I insisted he read a few books on child psychology if he was going to contribute so much to the lessons.) And he mixes it with praise and love. I've never seen a frog with a finer Suzuki spirit. For example, after expecting so much of young Constance he whispers in my ear again.

"Constance," I relay, "Fred says he really likes your tone now." He whispers again.

"Oh Fred," I add with delight, "what a nice thing to say. He says he really likes you a lot too, Constance!"

Being such a lovable frog, occasionally Fred wants some of my students to hold him too much and I have to make a rule that he must stay on the piano during the lesson. When the lesson has concluded and he has behaved himself properly, he is then allowed to be held and loved to his heart's content.

Fred enjoys traveling to workshops and institutes with me. In fact, few frogs have ever journeyed quite as much as he. It is amazing how his charm can evoke a smile and willing response from a previously tense youngster.

Each year at Christmas Fred enjoys taking a vacation (usually to Florida). I do not feel deserted, however, for I own a Merry Christmas Hop Frog who spends the month of December in my studio. He was a special gift, made by one of my Suzuki mothers. Sewed in colorful Christmas fabric, he is stuffed with rice in honor of Dr. Suzuki. When he is pleased with accomplishments, the bell on his tongue jingles. He's quite a plump little fellow and full of holiday spirit.

It is always nice to have Fred return after Christmas. Teaching with him is a real joy! In fact, a number of my Suzuki parents have purchased a Mississippi Hop Frog of their own to assist in their home practice. You might consider finding a Fred for yourself sometime. If you do, I hope he will have as many fine qualities as mine.

Chapter 6

Focus On Technique

Developing the Hand Position

Learning a natural hand position for the young pianist is not always an easy task. It is an important beginning procedure, however, for the child to see and understand how the hand, arm and fingers are to look while playing the piano.

At the child's first lesson I place a ball in the right hand to help give a feeling of shape to the hand. The size of the ball is important, for if it is to give the feel of a natural hand position which is somewhat arched but not too rounded, the ball must not be too small. I ask the child to hold the ball and I place the child's forearm in a position which is parallel to the floor. I then tell a very nonsensical story. The dialogue runs as follows:

"Stephannie, let's pretend that you, Mother and I are taking a trip in this special red and white car." (the pretend "car" is a felt-tip washable, red-ink pen I am holding while I move slowly along her arm to each area we discuss.) "We're going to start right here at your forearm and travel down your arm, which is a very straight road. As we cross your wrist in our car, notice how straight it is. We continue traveling on to your hand until we hit a bump in the road." (The bump is the big knuckle on our hand.) "Let's travel on to one of your fingers; there is another bump, and still another." (These are the joints in the fingers that the pen is now touching.) "These are the bumps that piano players have when they are playing the piano." We then discover that all the fingers have these same bumps in them.

Next we turn the hand over with the ball still in the hand. With the red pen, I mark dots on the fingers where they would naturally touch the keys. We discover that the thumb would touch on its side and carefully mark a dot beside the thumb nail to show its exact touching position.

On turning the hand back to normal position, the dots disappear. In order to have any appealing visual image for this position, I draw a small smiling face on the thumb.

Next the ball is removed from the hand and we try to maintain the same position as we place it on the piano. My red pen now becomes a kitty who tries to travel under the child's hand in the arch left by the ball. If it can travel under safely without being crushed, it comes out purring. If it is crushed as it travels under, it meows loudly.

During this entire process, 4-year-old Stephannie has listened attentively to every word and has understood because I have expressed it to her through a child's pretend story. She and her mother eagerly review the entire story at home and look daily for the straight road, the bumps, the thumb that touches beside the thumbnail, the smiling face, and the kitty who travels under the bridge. They repeat the procedure at least three times each day when they begin their practice in the early months of their lessons. Stephannie may not be able to maintain this position as she plays in the very beginning, but she has a clear picture of every detail toward which she is working and eventually it is maintained in her playing.

There is never a lesson during all of Book 1 in which I do not first look for this basic hand, arm and finger position. Stephannie places her hand in position at the piano as soon as proper posture is assumed. "Let me see," I say, "I see a straight road with three bumps on it. I like the way your thumb is touching beside the thumbnail."

"Don't forget to let the kitty go under the bridge," Stephannie exclaims as she looks at me with bright eyes and a big smile.

"All right," I reply as my pretend kitty travels under her bridge. "Oh, Stephannie, the kitty is purring!"

Learning to Read Notation

For years I have been hearing the criticism of individuals outside the Suzuki movement that Suzuki students do not learn to read music. I have thought to myself what a ridiculous notion it is. Of course they can learn to read music.

There is nothing inherent in the method or philosophy to prevent learning the reading of musical notation. It makes no more sense than to say the child who learned to talk first cannot learn to read when he begins first grade. In fact, my strong feeling is that Suzuki students can become the finest of readers because they are able to hear what they are reading.

But *are* they learning to read? I am cognizant of a rising concern among many of us who teach the method that our students are not developing as they should in this area. If the problem is not the method, then what is it?

There simply have to be other reasons. Could one of them be us—the teachers?

Somehow we are not producing enough good readers—sometimes in spite of our best efforts. We cannot assume total blame, however, for we know that children in other methods struggle to learn to read also. It is a difficult skill for all to learn—both traditional and Suzuki.

We must seek to find every possible way to assist, however. Let us examine some possibilities and options we have.

Take Plenty of Time in the Beginning

Suzuki is always telling us that the beginning is the most important. I believe this to be true when our students begin their reading books as well as when they begin Suzuki instruction.

My students generally begin reading books as an adjunct to their lesson in early Book 2. By then, I hope to have accomplished sufficient musical, technical, and physical results in Book 1 that they can maintain them without as much intensity provided in the lesson as was previously given. Thus, I can devote the time needed to start them successfully in their reading books. In the first few lessons, it is not uncommon to devote 15 to 20 minutes of a 30-minute lesson to reading. Later, once the groundwork is laid we can ease that time span and spend less lesson time with the reading.

Prepare Them for Success

Preparing them for success entails sending the child and parent home with such a clear understanding of their reading assignment that they cannot fail. This can be accomplished through our Suzuki one-step mastery. For example, the procedure for beginning each new piece might be:

1. Mark the Notes. Mark dashes under the notes in the score— ♩ or 𝅗𝅥 for their rhythmic value.

2. Tap the rhythm. Tap the rhythm, counting aloud at the same time.

3. Scan the Score. Look through the music and discuss all musical symbols (dynamics, tempo markings, slurs, staccatos, etc.)

4. Look for Steps and Skips. Look at the notes and study their direction—do they skip down, step up, or what?

5. Play. Play the piece, counting aloud as you play.

These may not be the same steps you would recommend. That is all right. The point is to know your steps and see that the parent gets them in writing. (Perhaps you will want to write them out, just to be certain). In this way there will be a solid procedure for practice at home. The parent should feel secure because she knows exactly how to approach the reading assignment.

Be Consistent

The next step is never to assume that the reading will continue to be prepared weekly unless you are consistent about checking it. Too many of us trust that our students will obediently practice their reading even though we do not hear it in the lesson. Such a viewpoint is an idealistic one, for it is not human to work hard in preparation and not be honored with a hearing of it.

Structure a Time for It in the Lesson

My love in teaching is spending the lesson time on the Suzuki material. Thus, I have to discipline myself to set aside the beginning of the lesson for the reading. When a great deal has been prepared, however, I often eliminate some of the material by asking the child to choose only his favorite pieces to play for me, or by simply choosing one piece from each page. In this way, I can quickly grasp how well he has prepared his assignment and is understanding new concepts without absorbing too much of the lesson time.

Choose a Reading Method Carefully

The Suzuki method does not give us a specific note-reading approach. It is left to the individual teacher to develop this. I consider an interval approach excellent. With these well-trained Suzuki ears, all the children need is a label for each interval and they can transmit what they hear to the printed notation. Many of the method books on the market today are good. Beware of some of the old-fashioned series through which you might have learned and look for more recent ones.

Give Supplementary Material when Needed

There are times when children seem to plateau in their reading skills, but the method book continues to progress in difficulty. When the reading book becomes a struggle, so does the mental attitude toward reading. This is a time for providing supplementary material until the child is ready to progress to harder steps in the reading method. Look for easier material for a while. Perhaps you can lend some books from you own library. Do not feel hesitant to take an extended period of time if needed. Poor attitudes improve simultaneously with less stress and more success in the reading.

There are other valid reasons for supplementing. Special seasons such as Christmas provide wonderful variety and joy in the reading. Numerous Christmas books are available on the market. (Unfortunately, there is less available in Hanukkah music.) Each year I have my students begin their Christmas music earlier and earlier in order to have more time to enjoy these pieces. They are tremendous motivation.

Other books such as simplified hymn arrangements can provide some of the same pleasures at other times in the year. Never overlook the value of duets. They are available in all levels of difficulty and give the additional pleasure of ensemble to the students.

Include Sight-Reading Material

The finest thing I have ever done for my student's reading development has been to place them in sight-reading books. To discuss this, we need to be clear in our distinction between "reading" and "sight-reading." In order to sight-read, the student must first be able to read. The reading assignment involves the learning of all new concepts, notations, etc. Since it includes new steps, it is more difficult. Consequently, pieces given as part of the reading assignment take more time and repetition to prepare. The sight-reading consists of musical material at an easier level which the student is challenged to play well in one reading. There are steps involved in this process, however, that I use to prepare them for success. They are as follows:

First, tap the rhythm on the wood of the piano, using the right hand to produce the rhythm of the treble staff and the left hand to produce the bass staff.

Then, look over the music. Identify and discuss every sign and symbol in the score. This includes the key signature, dynamic markings, phrase indications, etc. It also includes identifying recognizable chords such as tonic, dominant, sub-dominant, etc. when shown in the score.

Next, play silently over the surface of the keys as many times as needed to feel adequately prepared for all the challenges of the score.

Finally, play the piece in its entirety only once. If the first three steps are followed carefully, there is a strong possibility that the results of this final step will be as desired.

Sight-reading books generally come with short pieces, many as short as one line. I ask that my students sight-read one piece each day. At the lesson I do not check the material they sight-read during the week, but rather have them sight-read the next piece in the book for me.

Since using this process, I have seen a marked improvement in reading skills. The Suzuki process of one-step-at-a-time mastery is being followed. Over a period of time it is exciting to see that these small steps all merge into one cohesive skill for the students.

Determine the Length of the Assignment Carefully

Careful consideration needs to be given to each child's assignment in terms of the amount. Each child varies in what he can accomplish, so some bending for individual needs is certainly a necessity. However, the child who prepares only one page of reading weekly is hardly doing enough to get "off the ground" with his reading skills. We must be equally cautious not to overwhelm with the length, however.

We have to sense the attitude felt about the reading. If it is good, then we can guess we have judged properly for that child. If it is not good, then it is time to ask questions about the length of assignments. If cutting down on one piece each week relieves some stress and brings a healthier attitude, it is well worth the omission.

Transfer Reading to the Suzuki Literature

There is a point in every Suzuki child's development when he must begin merging his reading skills into the Suzuki literature. This point varies somewhat from child to child, but for my own students, I basically try to begin this transition at the beginning of Book 3. It is at about this point that mothers tell me they are becoming cross-eyed from trying to check for good fingerings as little fingers play faster on the sonatinas this book offers. The demands of the music seem to need two good sets of eyes on the score to meet its challenges.

Some children are eager to begin this transfer, while others are reluctant. Regardless of the kind of child you have, the merging must come in order to develop the total musician. In order to begin this transition I make a conscious effort to place the Suzuki score on the music rack at the lesson. Even though I continue to teach through demonstration, I also make a point to refer to the score as well. The merging can be done in small steps, such as pointing to an accent or fingering in the beginning to help create an awareness of the score. Certainly one would not expect the child to transfer to a total reading process immediately. However, over a period of time these skills will all be incorporated.

Stress Rhythmic Pieces

Rhythm has always been considered one of the most difficult skills to master in learning to read. Once the children have begun reading in the Suzuki literature, one could falsely assume that they are reading complex rhythms—such as those that occur in the Mozart *Sonata*, K330. However, they are not. We must remember that they are always listening to these pieces, so their ears are solving many of the rhythmic problems of the pieces for them. Thus, the strengthening of good rhythmic reading must come from a source other than the Suzuki literature.

My student's favorite source is jazz. A number of fine jazz collections are available on the market today, ranging from easy to difficult. It is an invaluable source of good rhythmic reading. I have become relentless in my efforts to foster these rhythmic needs through jazz sources.

Other reading books can also supply help in developing rhythmic skills, especially 20th-century literature. Whatever the source used, our responsibility is to make certain our students are understanding and mastering rhythmic reading at a level which matches their other musical skills.

Continue Reading Indefinitely

It is my belief that even Book 6 graduates should continue reading from sources other than repertoire that is being learned through the combination of listening and reading. In addition to the already-mentioned jazz and sight-reading books, hymns provide a wonderful source for reading four-part harmony. They also afford good pedal experience for the student.

Set High Goals in the Reading

Students can continue using their Suzuki-trained abilities in every way as they translate notation into live music. Concepts already developed of musical phrasing, tone, balance, etc. can be realized and applied by the children in their reading assignment. My challenge to my students is to discover all these on their own before bringing the assignment to their lesson. In this way we are going far beyond the basic goals of reading correct notes, fingerings, and rhythm. The student is thinking for himself and utilizing all his knowledge and musical skills from his Suzuki training. When one discovers on his own, real learning is taking place. High goals of this nature produce exciting results.

Let us all redouble our dedication and efforts to produce fine readers. We can help alleviate those concerns and attitudes that exist by showing that indeed, Suzuki students can learn to read!

Using a Metronome

"What is that over there?" Joshua interrupts his lesson because his eye has caught a glimpse of the metronome that sits on the piano in my studio. I am delighted to spur his curiosity regarding it because I know that the day will come before we complete Book 1 that I will want him to own and learn to use one.

"That's a metronome, Joshua. It won't be long before I'll want you to have one of your own," I reply. "Would you like me to save some time at the end of your lesson to show you how it works?" Joshua nods with bright and curious eyes. I am pleased because he has provided me an opportunity to plant the seeds of desire needed for his future success in using a metronome.

For years I have made a practice of questioning fine teachers of piano (both traditional and Suzuki) as to whether they assign practice with the metronome with their students. While some do not, a large number tell me they do.

Many students dislike using a metronome, however. A major part of their problem is that they do not know how to stay with the beat of the instrument; thus, it becomes a frustration. If we as teachers will take the time when they begin to help them learn to use it effectively, chances are that they will enjoy using it a great deal more.

When my students are approaching *Allegretto 2* with their hands together, I tell them to purchase a metronome if they do not already own one. My main requirement is that they seek one that has a loud tick, for some are too quiet to hear when playing. As with Joshua, I have taken a little time to motivate them about owning and using one so that they feel excited and honored to have reached the point that they are ready for this special new venture.

Here are the steps I use in helping my students learn to use the metronome:

1. Speak with the Tick at Various Speeds. Using two-syllable words (such as "tick-tock" or "jel-lo"), I move the metronome to various settings and we speak these words rhythmically with each tick. It is fun to see how we range from very slow speech at a metronome setting of 60 to extremely fast speech at 200.

2. Play the Piano with the Beat of the Metronome. Beginning at a setting such as 120, we again speak words to the beat; then we add the new step of playing to the beat immediately after speaking. The notes played are simply repeated notes on any given pitch.

3. Play to the Beat with _Allegretto 2._ I have enjoyed using _Allegretto 2_ for this first experience. Using a setting of about 132 to the eighth note, we begin by speaking aloud the beat as in step one, then playing the eighth note Gs of the first measure as our beat. Once the child has established the beat securely, I play the right hand melody of _Allegretto 2_ against his Gs. The child thus hears how the rhythm fits the beat he is playing.

4. Play the Actual Piece with the Metronome. "Now you are ready to play the piece yourself, Joshua," I say. "There is just one rule for you to follow before you begin. You must give a countdown. Let's say 'One, two, ready, play' in time with the metronome before we begin." This helps Joshua to establish the beat correctly and to begin rhythmically with the instrument. "One, two, ready play." pipes Joshua. And away he goes with the right hand of Allegretto 2 played in beautiful harmony with the metronome. To ensure his success I play along with him the first time. The next time I pat him lightly on his back to the beat as he plays alone. Then he plays it without any help from me. His eyes sparkle with pleasure as he finishes.

"You are terrific at staying with it, Joshua!" I exclaim. "That was so good I think we'll try it faster this time." Soon we are playing it several notches faster and have laid the groundwork for future success with the metronome in Book 2 where I like to use it extensively as a teaching tool.

Not every child will grasp the skill of using a metronome as quickly as Joshua did in one lesson. However, by patiently repeating these steps all students can eventually learn at their own pace, just as they learn all skills in the Suzuki method.

The next week Joshua grins as he tells me he has progressed in playing _Allegretto 2_ from 132 to a metronome setting of 152. Step by step his fingers have learned to increase their facility. They are controlled and even because of the gradual building process the metronome has given them.

It is obvious that Joshua has had a positive experience with his metronome practice. It has provided him with a sense of accomplishment. He likes playing faster, also. "Just think, Joshua," I smile in response, "you'll never get to go that fast in a car!"

Transposition

"For our next group lesson, let's be ready to transpose *Lightly Row* to the keys of A and B," I stated. "Continue the same procedure as you did for F and G today. Those were excellent." My class of children and parents nodded with a look of confidence and pleasure, for they completely understood and enjoyed the process we followed in order to transpose.

Transposition is a skill many present-day piano students learn. Numerous leading methods teach it; thus, many of our students gain some exposure to it through their reading books.

Our Suzuki students can gain additional experience with transposition when they finish Book 1 by using it as one way to maintain review of that book. Many of the Book 1 pieces are in five-finger positions with simple I, IV, and V chord harmonies—just the type of pieces needed for beginning transposition skills. Since the Suzuki repertoire utilizes mostly white keys (and with good reason), transposition provides our students the chance to begin some familiarity with other keys.

The Transposition Process

The process for learning transposition is a simple one. Let us take *Mary Had a Little Lamb* as our piece with which to begin and look at the necessary steps to follow:

1. First ask the student to play *Mary Had a Little Lamb*, as written in the key of C.

2. While his hand remains in the same position, have the child play the five notes over which the right hand is resting (C, D, E, F, G). Have him play both up and down this 5-finger pattern in a moderate quarter note rhythm.

3. Now have the child move his right hand to D and discover the same 5-finger pattern by sound. Here is an example of what might happen.

"Let's start on D and make it sound like the pattern we just played on C, Loren," I state. Loren does as told and looks surprised when it sounds different as he plays up the white keys.

"Something sounds different, doesn't it, Loren?" I smile. "This time let's play until we hear a note that sounds wrong. When we hear it, we'll stop on that note." Loren does as directed and plays D, E, F, and stops. The F, of course, is wrong. "Instead of the F, let's try a note nearby and see if we can find the correct sound,"

I suggest. With this suggestion in mind, Loren soon discovers that F-sharp sounds exactly right. He smiles with pleasure at his discovery.

Loren will not be quite as surprised as he discovers additional 5-finger patterns because he now realizes he might need a combination of white and black keys in order to find them. He is also discovering them by ear, which is strengthening his Suzuki-oriented learning. There will be time later in his development to understand the whole and half step arrangement.

4. Next, move the child's left hand to D and play the same 5-finger pattern. Now have him find the I and V chords in that key, again discovering them by sound.

5. When the child is comfortable with the last two steps (you might send him home for a week practicing steps three and four to give him ample familiarity in the new key), then have him play *Mary Had a Little Lamb*, keeping the fingers over the new position. Right hand will begin on the same finger on which it began in the original key.

Best-Suited Pieces

Some of the Book 1 pieces I have found best-suited for first experiences with transposition are *Mary Had a Little Lamb, Lightly Row,* and *Cuckoo*. These are in a 5-finger position and utilize mostly I and V chords in the left hand. *Little Playmates* is another easy one and offers the left hand a chance to become acquainted with the V7 chord in various keys.

Later, it is nice to add *Go Tell Aunt Rhody* for a piece which extends right hand a sixth rather than a fifth and gives the left hand an opportunity to learn the IV chord in new keys. *Allegro* provides an octave range for transposition, giving additional skills to the student.

Although there is no rule for the order of new keys in which to transpose, I generally have my students learn the white keys first and then the black keys. One or two new keys can be added when the child is ready for a new assignment. When these are secure, we move to new ones.

Both group and private lessons can work nicely for development of transposition skills. Since private lessons provide such a challenge for fitting in the development of all the needed skills, we could make a good case on that basis to use part of the group lesson for learning this skill. If this is done, home assignments for practice must still be made. Transposing with partners (one playing right hand and the other, left hand) can add to the fun of learning the skill.

Transposition can be started at any time. I always wait until my students begin

Book 2 so we can use it as another way to maintain Book 1 review. It is a skill I want all my Suzuki students to have at some point. I hope you will consider teaching it to your students also if you have not already done so.

Chapter 7

Focus On Musicality

Dynamics

As a piano student at the graduate level, I had difficulty in making quality dynamic changes on certain passages of music, especially those demanding sudden changes. My teacher used to tell me that I needed to improve my dynamics. I remember gulping and feeling terrible right down to the pit of my stomach, for I knew I needed better control of dynamics—I just did not know how to acquire that control. Soft passages were always the most difficult. At the time, I thought there was something wrong with me and my playing.

As I look back, I realize that my teachers throughout my training were much better at telling me *what* I needed to do than showing me how to achieve it. This realization has led me to a lifetime search in my own teaching to acquire techniques that show *how* to arrive at results in all areas of my students' development. I would like to share with you a few of the techniques that I utilize in working with dynamics.

Begin Through Demonstration

We are so fortunate in the Suzuki method that we begin all concepts through listening. In the area of dynamics, the student must first hear that levels of big, medium, and soft volume exist in the music. Dynamics are not difficult to hear, but nevertheless, an awareness of them must be present in order to begin executing them.

I always delay introducing varied dynamic levels with the beginning student until I know he can produce a consistently beautiful, full-bodied tone of a *mf* to f level of volume. Softer tones are more difficult, so they are a second step. When readiness is apparent, I use my follow the leader game for introducing the softer volumes. In doing so, I play a simple passage (such as C-D-E-F-G-G on *Twinkle A* rhythm) for the child at a *forte* level, which he will imitate for me. Then I repeat the identical passage at a *piano* level. Often the child plays the same notes but has not become sensitive yet to the change of dynamics. Rather than tell the child that it needs to be softer, I simply tell him that he did a good job playing the same notes as I and that this time I want him to listen for something special I did with the notes. It may take several times for the child to realize what he needs to change in his playing, but the process of helping the child learn through discovery is far better than telling him what to do, so I am willing to wait until he discovers it for himself.

The child's first attempts at playing softly usually result in some frustration, for soft tones are challenging to play. In the next weeks and months, I ask that the child and parent use some changing dynamics (*f* and *p* only at this point) with their follow the leader game at home to strengthen his ability. In the lesson, I continue to give at least one passage in our game that is *forte* and then *piano*. I also introduce through demonstration in the follow the leader game some crescendos and diminuendos, skills which additionally demand control of volumes. We use a simple five-finger pattern in the beginning to achieve our results. This generally requires less than a minute of the lesson, but it has provided me a chance to focus at least briefly on dynamics.

Awareness plus a small skill level is now present. Our Suzuki process of teaching through demonstration has been utilized. It should remain a key factor in working with dynamics and should be combined continually with the other suggestions that follow. It is the most important factor in achieving our results.

Use the Stop-Prepare Technique

The next step is to find techniques that help improve the quality of the dynamics. The stop-prepare technique is one of the most valuable. I learned to use it through teaching the Suzuki method, but how I wish my own teachers had known to use it with me.

A few years ago I was reading an article in a piano periodical by a concert pianist who discussed the value of stopping when practicing between sudden dynamic changes in order to gain control. I went to my piano and tried it on a difficult Chopin *Nocturne* that had several such demands in it. For a few days, I practiced stopping at those difficult points just long enough to relax and prepare myself mentally and physically for the new dynamic level. It was wonderful! I soon found that I had the control I had needed for years. Since that time, I have been in full awareness of the value of that word STOP and I constantly show my own students how to do this in their practice. I mark the word at the appropriate places in their scores, we practice the technique in the lesson, and I send them home with the assignment to do the same several times a day in their home practice. The results have been exciting.

Shadow-Play the Soft Passages

Since soft playing is the most difficult volume of playing, techniques to improve that dynamic level are especially needed. One of the finest I have found is to shadow-play these passages. Shadow-playing is the process by which the student plays the passage silently on the surface of the keys. I enjoy telling my students that we are "ghosting" because it sounds as silent as a ghost would if he were playing the piano.

An example in the literature where such a procedure is helpful is the third score of *Little Playmates*. In this, the child would play with a strong tone for the first two measures, STOP, and then ghost the next two measures. Once we have ghosted it, we then play the identical passage softly. The results and control from this are amazing. Shadow-playing need not be limited to beginning students as a technique. All levels can benefit from such practice.

Use Creative Techniques and Analogies

With the young child, in particular, the use of the words "loud" and "soft" are boring and lacking in personality. (I have a difficult time tolerating the word "loud" as an explanation of *forte* for any level student, for I feel it connotes a harsh, ugly sound.) It is far more interesting and effective to use colorful words and techniques to help motivate interest in dynamics.

A favorite game to arouse interest in dynamics with a young student is to turn him into a vending machine. This vending machine has two buttons on it—a big one and a soft one. First I deposit some pretend money in his head so that the machine will work. When I push his right leg, it makes the "big" or *forte* button work; his left leg is for the "soft" or *piano* button.

The vending machine idea works well with *Allegretto 1*. If the child flounders with one of his dynamic levels, I complain that the vending machine is not working properly. Mother understands how to play the game at home, so she and the child play it until we reach our goal—that the vending machine learns to work automatically! As a result, the child who was previously bored with a more pedantic approach is now thrilled and alert.

Another favorite analogy (not original with me) is the use of "brother-sister" dynamics. For example, in a piece such as *Christmas Day Secrets* I have the child choose the person who would be the noisier at his house on Christmas day. He can choose as it relates best to his own family, whether it be a brother, sister, dad, or the dog. The noisier person then becomes the one singing or talking on the *mp* passages and the other child takes the *p* passages. Combining this colorful idea with a STOP between each passage for a week of home practice brings excellent results even from three and four-year-olds.

Even at the most advanced levels, the use of more colorful terminologies than "loud" and "soft" is strongly recommended. A real turning point for me in my own concept of dynamics came one summer when I studied a Mozart sonata with a concert pianist who projected the idea to me that I not think in terms of louds and softs, but rather in orchestral colors. I spent the next few days in ecstasy over the thrill of having my fingers produce flutes, trumpets, full orchestras, *etc.,* in that piece of music!

Since then I have filled my own music and my students' with such thoughts. The opening chord of the Book 4 Beethoven *Sonata,* Op. 49, No. 2 is presented as though Beethoven is conducting a large orchestra, producing a rich, resonant, full sound. The Bach *Musette* begins the first two measures with a light flute playing, followed by a trumpet in the next two measures. It has been fun and the results have shown imagination and color in their dynamic effects.

Allegro con brio

With young children who are often not familiar with orchestral sounds, other analogies can work equally well. For example, the opening eight measures of the Kuhlau *Sonatina,* Op. 55, No. 1 Vivace movement can be portrayed as sounds of a baby bunny, thus giving a spirit of lightness as well as staccato effects to the music. The following phrase (which is identical except that it is f) can be the daddy bunny.

55

Dance forms in the literature can represent mothers or dads dancing for the bigger dynamic levels and perhaps children for the softer, lighter passages. Sequences involving rising dynamic levels can be projected to the little person as baby, mommy, and daddy sizes. This is a concept even a very young child can understand.

The use of crescendos and diminuendos, another form of dynamics, can be helped through the use of imagery. For example, the left hand scale section of *Short Story* can be part of a grand story about a birthday party. In this part, the ascending scales of the left hand represent the footsteps of the boys and girls as they approach the party from a distance. They begin softly and grow bigger as they come closer. As they approach (measure 12), mother exclaims that everyone is too noisy, so they step softly again (measure 13) until, alas, the children forget mother's request and become noisy again. Not only are my students sparked by such analogies, but my own teaching is also. Dynamics, as well as the piece, come to life.

Reverse Dynamics for Practice

At a more advanced level, reversing dynamics on certain passages is beneficial as a practice technique. For example, sometimes huge fortes needed on big chordal passages can create tension in the hands and arms. Practicing these passages softly can help relax these tensions. On the other hand, soft passages can often sound weak and lacking in singing tones. These passages can be helped by forte practice where it is easier to play into the key beds.

Adjust Height for Dynamic Control

In certain passages (such as measure 17 of *Arietta*) where the arm can drop on the notes from above the keys as we play, the height of the arm can help control the dynamic level. If we dropped a heavy book on the floor from a height of 12 inches, it would produce a substantial thud; if we dropped the same book from an inch above the floor, the sound would be considerably less. The same principle can apply to dropping from a higher arm for *forte* passages and one closer to the keys for *piano* passages. A higher hand elevated from the wrist and a higher finger operate the same way, giving more volume to the tone.

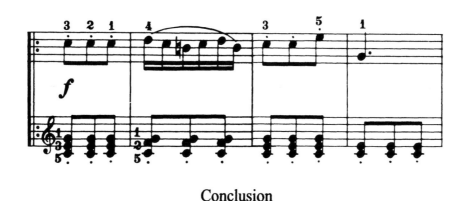

Conclusion

The suggestions given in this article are a few among many techniques used for producing good dynamics. They are by no means complete, nor are they all totally original.

It is my hope that we all continue to search for fine ways to bring music to life with our students. Through the use of demonstration, imagination, and good techniques, our students can move a long way toward projecting beautiful dynamics.

Balance

Regardless of its difficulty, musical balance between the hands is a skill that the Suzuki pianist can and should begin very early in his development. Book 1, with its many melodic folk tunes, demands a focus on balance if we are to achieve complete mastery of each piece.

From the onset of his study, the Suzuki child has the decided advantage of hearing and absorbing good balance through listening to his recording or tape. The groundwork for good balance can be laid at the piano as well, even before the hands are played together on the piece. Parents should be instructed to play the left hand accompaniment lightly while the child is playing fuller tones on the right-hand melody. When the child begins the left hand, he should also be instructed to play it lightly while the parent plays the right hand. In this way, the child is benefiting from listening to good balance at his instrument as well as on his tape in the earliest stages of his development.

When is it Time?

When the child first puts his hands together on *Cuckoo* he is attempting to coordinate two hands, and it is premature to ask for balance. The skilled teacher will recognize the point and time at which the child overcomes this difficulty. As the child reaches *Go Tell Aunt Rhody*, he will most likely display much greater ease in coordination, and the time will be ripe to introduce balance to his pieces.

Creating a mental awareness in the child of what it means to have balance is helpful. Children have responded with much understanding and delight to an analogy I have drawn between musical balance and a teeter-totter. I put both my hands in front of me, holding them level as a balanced teeter-totter should be. We then have the left hand represent the child on a teeter-totter and the right hand represent Mother or Dad. The child enjoys pushing the left hand up and the right hand down to show what happens to the teeter-totter under such unequal weights. I tell the child that the right hand should be overweighted when playing the piano. In this way, he realizes that good balance on the piano is not like good teeter-totter balance at all.

Teaching Ideas

With such a clear picture in the child's mind, we proceed to practice balance on the piano. One excellent technique involves having the child play the left hand of a piece silently over the top of the keys while the right hand is ringing out its melody in big, full tones. When the child is asked to play the left hand a little "bigger" so that it makes a very quiet sound, he has such a fine feel for playing lightly from the "silent" exercise that many times the proper balance between the hands is accomplished immediately. The skill of balancing hands may not be a permanent part of his technique at this point, but it has its beginnings. The "silent" exercise can be repeated over and over again until balance does become a part of the child's pianistic skills.

A different but effective technique for hearing and achieving balance is playing the piano with crossed hands. For instance, in pieces with right hand melody, move the left hand up an octave higher than usual to play its part. Then cross the right hand over the left to play below it. This position softens the strokes of the left hand quite naturally, and the child is able to hear a strong difference in the hands. Needless to say, other benefits, such as improved concentration, are gained from this technique also.

A third method that helps teach balance is asking the child to play the first left-hand chord or note of a piece quietly, placing his hand on top of the key as it begins. This can be repeated a number of times until the quiet tone needed is well established and is easily played. The right hand can then bring in its first note immediately after the left hand's, but should drop from above the key in order to achieve the bigger tone needed. Parents feel a great deal of confidence in working at home with this approach because they can hear the difference in the hands more easily when first one hand is played and then the second one is added.

The Suzuki teacher can give additional help by demonstrating good balance for the child in the lessons. A good listening exercise for her to use is to play a phrase of a piece for the child two ways: one with a heavy left hand and the other with well-balanced hands. From this, the child not only can hear and choose the example which is best, but he also begins to recognize how unattractive unbalanced music is in comparison. This helps instill a desire in him to play music the more beautiful way. This listening approach should be used by the teacher from the very beginning of her focus on balance.

Choice of Literature

Certain pieces in the Book 1 literature lend themselves to early success in achieving balance. *Mary Had a Little Lamb* is an excellent piece for a first attempt, and *Chant Arabe* is another good choice. In both pieces, the left hand is not as active as it is on the alberti and broken chord accompaniments found in much of the other literature. Success in one piece breeds success in other, more difficult ones. Soon, balance between hands can become a skill of every piece.

The good Suzuki student should hear balance and desire it in his playing. It is one of many of the fine skills to be pursued in Book 1 to help him meet the new challenges of the books that follow.

Phrasing

One of the earliest theorists to write on the subject of phrasing described it as "the most remarkable and least noticed aspect" of musical language. How fortunate we are that our Suzuki students have the advantage of hearing and absorbing good musical phrasing through their listening. There are also a number of valuable teaching techniques we can utilize to further stress and implement good phrasing with our students from the beginning of their instruction.

The subject of phrasing encompasses two main areas. The first relates to the division of the musical line into parts. The second relates to the handling of the content of the phrase.

Phrase Division

Let us look first at the area of division of the parts and discuss techniques for strengthening that aspect of phrasing in our teaching. From the very beginning we teach our pieces by phrases. For example, the A section of *Twinkle A* is learned well before continuing to the B section. As a result, the child hears the music in parts.

As we continue through the literature and turn the learning of the notes over to the parents, we can continue to mark the music into parts. Before sending mother and child home to begin the new piece we can say "Mother, let me mark the phrases for you. Be sure Bobby knows each part well before continuing to the next part." Numbers can be given to each phrase so that the child learns the first phrase as "part one," the second phrase as "part two," *etc.*. Mother can make more sense of the new piece from the beginning by knowing its proper divisions.

The "Scramble" card game presented by Bigler and Watts in *Studying Suzuki Piano* is a wonderful tool for strengthening phrasing. Each phrase is again named by a number such as part one, two, or three. After the child knows the piece well in its parts he is ready to play the game. Aces, twos, and threes from a deck of cards are mixed and the player draws one of the cards from the teacher or parent. Whichever part is drawn must be played. The game continues until all cards have been drawn. Extra cards for parts needing more repetition can be used. This game can be taught from the first *Twinkle* variation and can give much fun and repetition while strengthening phrasing concepts as well.

The "peanut butter and jelly sandwich," also introduced by Bigler and Watts, serves as another excellent aid to strengthen concepts of phrasing in the beginning of instruction. The A section of *Twinkle* becomes the bread while the B section is the peanut butter and jelly. What fun it is to hear the parts creatively!

To help the child focus on lifting off the keys for phrasing needing separations, the teacher or parent can have the child put his hands in his lap between each phrase. Since the student has already learned the piece in parts, it is an easy matter to ask the child to stop at the end of each part and put his hands in his lap. I usually demonstrate by doing it first for the child. Putting hands in the lap forces one to concentrate on the phrase ending. Once the child is able to achieve this, the next step is to have the child stop at the end of each phrase by merely lifting the hand slightly from the keys instead of going to the lap. The final step is to achieve the lift rhythmically, without any stops. *Allegretto 2* is a good example of a piece divided into four phrases where it is effective to have both hands lift in order to breathe between the parts.

Some phrases need only one hand lifted while the other connects. For example, *Allegretto 1* sounds lovely with only a right hand lift after the first eight measures. The stop-prepare technique at such a place is most valuable to achieve this result. After stopping, the left hand must hold its note while the right hand lifts. Fun on the lift can be added by having the right hand either wave to mother, rub the tummy, or pat the head. Soon the independence of hands needed for this type of phrasing becomes easier.

Other phrases can be felt and achieved without any lifts. Care must be given on the part of the teacher in determining the kind of phrasing needed to meet the demands of the music.

Phrase Content

The second area of phrasing, that of handling the content of the phrase, is one that contributes to the meaningful shaping of the melody. It involves, according to the *Harvard Dictionary of Music*, "proper accentuation, variety of attack and subtle crescendos and decresendos."

A musical means for both teacher and child to help determine the proper arch of the phrase is to sing it or dance to it. For a more comprehensive and scholarly guide, the following two principles are recommended by William S. Newman in *The Pianist's Problems:*

> 1. In a phrase that contains some unusual feature, that feature becomes the climactic point. The feature may be an unusually expressive harmony, remote foreign tone, long tone, high tone, low tone, or an unexpected dynamic marking, provided that it occurs in a way that permits adequate emphasis...

> 2. Otherwise the climactic point of the phrase normally occurs on the last strong beat before the final note. The strong beat, in this sense, is usually the first beat of the measure...William S. Newman, *The Pianist's Problems: A Modern Approach to Efficient Practice and Musicianly Performance* (New York: Harper & Row, 1956). pp 95-96.

I have always appreciated Pablo Casals' choice of the word "rainbow" to describe the subtle *crescendos* and *descrescendos* involved in shaped phrases. The rainbow concept can be introduced early in the child's training through a listening approach. I enjoy making my students cognizant of them as they are advancing in their "Twinkles." Through a copycat game I play a pattern of C-D-E-F-G-F-E-D-C on the piano for them, allowing the rainbow I am presenting to peak on the G.

The child usually plays back the same notes correctly, but without the rainbow on the first attempt. "Good for you, Bobby," I say, "you played the correct notes. Now listen again for something more." At this point I repeat the pattern, giving a very exaggerated rainbow. Bobby smiles this time, for he has heard something special in the notes. He tries to reproduce it but finds it difficult. It is time for me to break it into smaller steps. I play only the first note, very softly and on the *Twinkle A* rhythm, and then on a single note. Bobby answers with the same. Next I play the high G in the same manner with a very big tone. Bobby can also do this. I then play the first half of the rainbow with a big crescendo from C to G. Bobby is somewhat successful in his attempt. We then practice the big tone on G, the soft tone of C, and decrescendo from G to C on the second half of the rainbow. It is fun to discover that we have made a rainbow.

An assignment is made to begin practicing the rainbow on those same notes, daily, but dividing it in the two parts at first. Rainbow attempts can be awkward and difficult for students in the beginning, but with daily practice they become more and more a skill. I check them weekly in the lesson through our copycat game. As I see them becoming easy for the student, we can begin to incorporate some of them into our Suzuki pieces.

There is a visual aid my students have enjoyed in helping refine their rainbows. On a piece of paper I draw two kinds of rainbows that people play. They look like this:

Rainbow number two always draws a laugh or a curious expression. We then proceed with a listening game where I play a rainbow and ask the child to show me which picture I am playing. When the first rainbow is played, it is beautifully rounded at the top. Rainbow number two is not nearly as lovely for it simply has one big note that sticks out most unattractively above the rest. Once the child hears the difference he begins to refine his own rainbows toward the more beautiful first version.

Some other aspects of the phrase can also be dealt with early in training. For example, larger phrases sometimes divide into smaller units. Within the smaller units are often found sequences, such as in phrase three of *Lightly Row* (measures 9-12). To help the child hear these sequences brings understanding of the music and consequently intelligent playing at a very early age. These sequences can be presented through analogies such as "families." The child and I decide that since the group of notes (sequence) following the first pattern or family of notes is so very much like it, this second family must be related to the first. Thus, they can become "cousins" to one another. Other times in the literature there are sequences which can give interest to the phrase by varying the dynamic level of each. Sequences giving a nice effect with a crescendo can be approached as baby, mommy, and daddy sizes. Phrases which repeat the same pattern, such as the B section of *Twinkle A* and *Honeybee,* can be varied on the repeat with a possible echo.

Certain phrases gain beauty by stressing special notes. Some of the minuets of Book 2 can be made quite beautiful by stressing or leaning into the quarter notes on first beats of the measures. Excellent examples of this are measures five, six, and seven of *Minuet 1*. It is fun to put the child back into the 18th century by pretending that a girl is in a long beautiful gown with a hoop skirt dancing the minuet or that a boy is in a powdered wig, ruffled shirt, knickers,and knee socks. As they "dance" through these measures of *Minuet 1*, they most definitely are bowing or leaning over as they emphasize those special quarter notes of each little phrase.

Other special notes within a phrase sometimes need a great deal of warmth. I call these "love notes" and draw a heart around them in the score. This means they are to be treated with special love and warmth when played. Lesson time is spent learning to hear the kind of warmth needed. I play and have the child listen to help determine the desired sound. My examples range from beautiful to poor in quality, thus helping the child learn to discriminate between them. "How was that one, Bobby?" I might ask. Bobby gives answers such as "good—full of love—not so good—it sounded a little angry—that one was beautiful." We then reverse the process as I evaluate the quality of Bobby's notes. Once Bobby hears the desired sound, it becomes easier to reproduce on his own.

People who hear young Suzuki pianists play are amazed at the beauty of their playing. At the same time, they often question whether the children really know what they are doing or if they are simply copying a recording. It is possible to build an understanding of music from the beginning with these children. Our work with phrasing can contribute greatly to this overall understanding. We can begin the process while teaching the *Twinkle* variations.

Tempo

How many of us have had a student with the ability to play a piece very beautifully, only to spoil its performance by a poorly chosen tempo or an unsteady tempo? This occurs frequently and is a difficult pedagogical problem to handle, but it does need to be addressed and solved. The time to begin the focus on tempo is in Book 1, while the groundwork is being laid for the child's success and high standards are being set for books to come. A steady and well-chosen tempo is a prerequisite to successful playing.

The Book 1 child in the Suzuki method is typically a pre-school child, so there is a strong need for the teacher to be creative and to capture the child's interest in this area. Certainly no three- or four-year-old is going to respond to any comment as dull as "You are not keeping a steady tempo," or "You must slow down."

Listening Games

I have found a few listening games and creative approaches with my pre-schoolers that have helped a great deal in focusing on tempo. Since listening is at the core of the Suzuki philosophy, this first game relates beautifully. My students play tonalization for me at every lesson; it is a chance to focus not only on beautiful tone and legato, but also on maintaining an even, steady tempo. I always ask my parents to close their eyes to see if they can tell us apart while first I play tonalization and then the child.

The parent is not told, of course, that I'll be playing first, but I always do so that the child can model after me. Often the parent might say after listening that "They both sounded very beautiful, but I thought maybe Sarah played second because fourth finger was a little weaker in the second player." There are also many times when the parent says, "I thought Sarah must have played second because that person started playing faster before she finished."

This gives me a chance to say that maybe if Sarah and I played the same tempo, Mother could not tell us apart as easily. Sarah wants to try again, which we do, and this time Mother has much greater difficulty telling us apart. As you might guess, when the tempo stabilizes so does the tone quality and legato. This listening game need not be confined to tonalization, but can be applied to passages in the literature for years to come.

Animal Stories

Children relate well to animals and animal stories. To make a child aware of various tempi that can be chosen for a piece, we often try the piece at the speed of certain animals. "Turtle" speeds give us the chance to play the piece very slowly.

Deer running very gracefully give us not only a feel for a more moderate speed, but for a certain mood of gracefulness we might hope to achieve. Running dogs are often chosen for the faster *tempi*. Bunny rabbits, grasshoppers and elephants are other animals that can be initiated to help establish a combination of tempo and a feeling for the spirit of the piece. After experimenting with different *tempi*, the child and I then determine the particular animal that best fits the mood and tempo of the piece.

In order to establish a habit of slow practice on a fast piece, I add that the piece needs to be practiced at "turtle tempo" several times a day in order to be very beautiful. Pretend "turtle pills" are handed to Mother to administer to the child for the slow practice, or to be given if the tempo begins rushing while the child is playing.

Speeding Tickets

Playing "policewoman" with the child has been another effective way of focusing on tempo problems. After making sure that the child understands that policewomen and policemen can give tickets for speeding or for going too slowly, I pretend to be a policewoman who really enjoys giving tickets. We determine if the speed limit for the piece needs to be 25, 50, or 80 miles per hour. I then send the child home with the assignment of trying to stay within the speed limit of that piece so they will not receive a ticket from me when they return the following week. The challenge is such fun for them that I have never had to give one of my "tickets," and the focus on a well-chosen, steady tempo has been achieved.

Use of the Metronome

As the child moves into Book 2, use of the metronome can be effective if well-handled. Metronome assignments ranging from slow to fast help build habits of steady practice on a piece and can also encourage many repetitions. On pieces that adapt themselves to this technique, I give the child and mother a metronome marking that is to be their goal for a performance tempo on a particular piece, and then give regular weekly assignments working toward the goal. Usually a minimum of five metronome markings ranging from slow to faster is given for each day's practice. The child develops the habit of playing steadily and enjoys seeing his progress as he increases the speed on the metronome. Controlled playing develops from this type of practice, as well as steady playing.

Use of the metronome does not guarantee a steady performance, however. When the desired performance tempo is achieved, care must be taken that the child is not dependent on the metronome to set his performance tempo or to maintain steadiness throughout the performance.

An effective way of helping the child know his tempo is to ask that he and mother reverse the procedure of setting the metronome first and then playing. The goal is to help the child memorize his performance tempo by beginning the piece and having mother turn on the metronome after he has played a few measures. This enables the child to see how close he came to establishing the prescribed tempo.

Focus of this kind, done several times during a practice period, is especially effective close to the time for a performance. To check steadiness of tempo within the piece, mother can turn the metronome on periodically during the playing of the composition—especially focusing on spots where there might be a tendency to rush or slow down.

Dr. Suzuki says that children have very wonderful minds. Indeed they do—even wonderful enough to conquer that age-old problem of tempo. The results will come from a combination of effective listening and effective teaching, and we will be another step closer to our goal of complete mastery of the Suzuki literature.

Chapter 8
Focus on Musical Periods

Group lessons can provide an excellent opportunity to acquaint students with knowledge of the various composers and styles of music. Students who have reached Book 2 in the Suzuki piano literature are becoming familiar with such names as Bach, Mozart, and Beethoven. Group lessons can provide a chance for interesting stories of the composers' lives; these can be told by the teacher or given as reports by the students.

I would like to share a story and game about Bach and the Baroque period which was enjoyed by a number of my students in a group lesson. This is by no means an attempt to cover all aspects of the styles of the Baroque, but is intended as a first step to acquaint young students with some aspects of the period which particularly pertain to keyboard music.

Before beginning the story in the group lesson, I challenged both students and parents to listen carefully so they could be ready for a game which would follow. As I told the story to the group, I asked one parent to write on a chalkboard the words which are in italics in the story. At the conclusion of the story, we reviewed those special words. The board was then erased and parents and children were divided into two teams for questions to see how much they had learned.

Introducing the Baroque

The Baroque Period: A Little Story

Johann Sebastian Bach was one of the greatest composers in the history of music. He did everything in a big way—he even had 21 children! Bach lived in the country of *Germany* at a time in history known as the *Baroque period*. The dates of the Baroque period were from *1600* to *1750*, a time when the colonies were being settled in America. Bach himself was born in 1685 and brought the Baroque period to a close with his death in 1750.

The keyboard instruments for which Bach wrote his music were not the piano, but the *harpsichord, clavichord* and *organ*. These instruments were beautiful to hear, but you could not play a forte or piano on them by the way you touched and depressed the keys as we can on the piano. These instruments were able to achieve changes in dynamics only by setting up certain buttons (called stops on the organ) in advance of playing or by having two or more keyboards of various dynamic levels. Often a section of a piece would be played on a forte keyboard and then repeated as an echo on a keyboard set up to achieve a piano effect.

Because it was necessary to achieve dynamics this way in the Baroque period, they were called *echo dynamics* or *terrace dynamics*. This became an important keyboard style of Bach's time.

Why didn't Bach write for the piano? The piano is the youngest of the keyboard instruments. It was invented during Bach's lifetime. Bach is said to have heard a piano and disliked it very much. This is because it was so new and many improvements still had to be made for it to sound beautiful as we know it today. It was years later when Mozart and Beethoven were alive that the piano was improved to the extent that these men really enjoyed writing music for it.

There are other interesting facts about the music in Bach's day. How many of you know what an *ornament* is? Do any of you put some ornaments on your Christmas tree? What do they do to the tree—give it an extra touch and sparkle, and extra decoration? Baroque composers like Bach enjoyed adding ornaments to their music. (At this point I played *Minuet* 3 from Book 2 and had everyone raise their hands when they heard the extra ornaments I added).

A last fact to share with you about Baroque music is that it is called *polyphonic music*. The word polyphonic means "many sounds." It can be compared to sounding as though two or more voices were singing different parts together. For example, *Minuet 1* could be thought of as the women or girls singing the upper (right hand) part, and the men or boys singing the left-hand part. When we play this music, we sometimes enjoy hearing the women's part emphasized and at other times, the men's part. The parts or voices even breathe in different places at times. (At this point I played the *G Minor Minuet* at the end of Book 2 to illustrate these points.)

A Quiz on the Baroque

1. What composer have we just discussed? (*J.S. Bach*)

2. In what period of history did he live and write? (*Baroque*)

3. What were the dates of this period? (*1600-1750*)

4. When was Bach born? (*1685*)

5. In what country? (*Germany*)

6. Name some keyboard instruments for which he wrote.
(*harpsichord, clavichord, organ*).

7. What kind of dynamics were used on these instruments? (*echo or terrace dynamics*)

8. Did Bach know a piano existed? (*Yes*)

9. What did he think about it? (*he disliked it*)

10. What can you tell me about Baroque music that was added to make it especially lovely at times? (*ornaments*)

11. What is polyphonic music? (music with more than one "voice" line)

It is always nice to make both teams winners by having the score come out even. Extra questions based on the story could be added at this point if needed to achieve this result.

An effective follow-up to this story and game is to ask everyone to play a Bach composition for the next group lesson. The teacher can help each child add a simple ornament or two in his piano lesson prior to the group lesson. (Children love adding ornaments to their music.)

If a harpsichord is available for use in the area, the next group lesson could be held at its location, giving everyone an opportunity to play his Bach composition on the harpsichord. If it has two manuals [keyboards], then repeats can be taken on the second manual for the echo effect.

My groups have enjoyed such activities as these. As a result, I can see them growing step by step toward a greater understanding of the goals we are striving to hear and achieve in our music.

Introducing the Classical Period

As a way of introducing the elements of the Classical Period, I would like to share a story and game about Beethoven and this period which I have used with my students in a group lesson. Certainly no other period of music could be more relevant to our Suzuki students than the Classical considering the large body of literature they study from that period. As described above in the section on the Baroque Period, I by no means attempt to cover all aspects of the Classical style. This story is simply an effort to familiarize them with some characteristics of the period, most especially those which pertain to the keyboard.

I begin by challenging both students and parents (be sure to include them— they love it) to listen carefully in order to be ready for a game to follow the story. As I tell the story to the group I ask one parent to write on a chalkboard the words which are in italics in my story. At the conclusion of the story, we review those special words. The board is then erased and parents and children are divided into two teams for questions to see how much they learned.

The Classical Period: The Story

Ludwig van Beethoven was one of the greatest composers in the history of music. He was born in 1770 in the European country of Germany. As a young boy his father told him about the wonderful musician and composer named *Mozart* who was 14 years older than he and quite famous. Beethoven admired Mozart greatly and wrote much of his earlier music in the same style. Beethoven undoubtedly heard about the composers *Haydn* and *Clementi,* for they, also, were well known in the musical world of his day.

That musical world later became known as the *Classical* period of music. It began about *1750* and ended around *1825*, a 75-year period. In America this overlapped the time of George Washington, the American Revolution, and the Declaration of Independence.

The Classical period was an exciting time for the piano, for it saw the rise and improvement of this instrument. Do you remember the terrace dynamics we discussed in the Baroque period? Because of the construction of the Baroque keyboard instruments, performers could only make dynamic changes by levels or terraces. With the invention of the piano, however, *changes in volume* with *crescendi* and *decrescendi* were possible to create by varying the weight in the depression of the keys. Beethoven was the first composer to write solely for the piano, for Mozart and Haydn had spend a lot of their time playing and composing for the clavichord and harpsichord.

Beethoven begged the piano makers of his day to continue improving the piano, for he played in such a big manner that he frequently broke the strings. It is said, in fact, that people dreaded inviting him to play in their home because he left their pianos in such a mess. Improve the piano was exactly what they did and it soon had a more beautiful tone. It was also capable of producing a far wider range of dynamics than had ever been known before. Beethoven used this potential of the new pianos by writing pieces which called for a *broader range of dynamics* than had been used by any other keyboard composers before him.

During Beethoven's lifetime he not only expanded the range of dynamics but he also began noting the dynamics he wanted in detail on his scores for the publishers. He marked slurs and staccatos in his compositions more carefully than had ever been done before. Publishers became aware of the composer's intended dynamics in detail for the first time. Composers before him had left a great deal more to the improvisation and discretion of the performer.

The Classical period was a time when all the keyboard composers wrote using special forms of music for their compositions. Among the most popular was the *sonata-allegro* form. Almost all first movements of the sonatas and sonatinas were written in that form. *Rondos* were another popular form of the day. These were frequently used in the last movements of sonatinas and sonatas. The composers followed strict rules in writing these musical forms.

The *Alberti bass* was a commonly heard figure in Classical keyboard compositions. (At this point I play the beginning of the Mozart *Sonata,* K545 to illustrate Alberti bass.) When a person hears a clear Alberti bass pattern in a fine composition, he can venture a good guess that it is from the Classical period, especially if most of the harmonies used with it are fairly simple, such as I and V chords.

Another interesting fact to share with you is that the Classical period began the use of *homophonic* music. In the Baroque, the harmony was polyphonic, meaning the music sounded as if two or more voices were singing together at the same time. With homophonic music, we begin to hear music that sounds as if one soloist is singing while the rest of the music is accompanying that solo. Most of the music that Suzuki pianists have played since Book 1 is homophonic. (At this point I play *Mary Had A Little Lamb* and *Lightly Row* to illustrate this melody and accompaniment style. At the same time I ask the class what they hear in the left hand of *Lightly Row.*)

Beethoven wrote music in the finest Classical style. However, due largely to the sad fact that he became deaf in later years, he began to turn toward a different style of writing that led us into a new period of music called the *Romantic* period. It will be fun to explore this period at another time.

The Quiz

1. Name the composer we have just discussed. (*Ludwig van Beethoven*)

2. In what period of music did he live and write? (*Classical*)

3. What were the dates of this period? (*1750-1825*)

4. Name the most important keyboard instrument of the Classical period. (*the piano*)

5. Name three other famous keyboard composers of the Classical period. (*Mozart, Haydn and Clementi*)

6. What was one thing the piano was capable of producing that the keyboard instruments before it could not? (*changes in volume with crescendi and diminuendi controlled by the depression of the keys.*)

7. What did Beethoven do for the dynamic range of the piano?
(*He expanded it greatly*)

8. Name two popular forms of writing of the Classical composers.
(*Sonata-allegro and rondo*)

9. Name a familiar pattern used in the harmonies by Classical composers.
(*the Alberti bass*)

10. Describe homophonic music. (*Music that has a solo melody and accompaniment.*)

11. What happened to Beethoven in his later years of life that contributed to his turning to a new style of composing? (*he became deaf.*)

12. What was the new period into which he led us called? *(Romantic)*

Conclusion

It is always nice to make both teams winners by having the score come out even. Extra questions based upon the story could be added at this point if needed to achieve this result.

After the group is acquainted with the Baroque and Classical periods of music, it is effective at later group sessions to follow up by playing unknown compositions in the two styles allowing the students to guess which style they hear. Bach two-part Inventions make excellent and relatively easy to identify examples of polyphony. Be sure to include an Alberti bass in the Classical example. Each child can also begin to announce the period of music he will play along with the title and composer when he performs at the group lesson.

It is exciting to provide this type of training to my students! How many educated adults are able to listen to fine music and understand as much about its style as these simple lessons have revealed to our students? It is another gift we can pass to our Suzuki students that will enrich their lives and perhaps stimulate them to learn even more. It also leads them to a deeper and richer understanding of the music they are playing.

Chapter 9
Focus on Effective Teaching

All of us can benefit from reevaluating our teaching skills and techniques. Here are some questions to help you do so; they were designed to help you examine the effectiveness of your teaching.

Are your students playing their Twinkles a tempo?
From the very beginning, it is important to work to play the *Twinkles a tempo.* Dr. Suzuki has said we must discard the idea that children cannot play fast. Just as children learn to speak their mother tongue at the same speed as adults, they can also play fast from the beginning provided their hands and arms are loose and relaxed.

Are you constantly calling out ideas to remember as the child is trying to play a piece for you?
In the Suzuki method, we endorse the idea of teaching one point at a time to achieve a step-by-step mastery. If you are calling out several ideas to remember as the child is playing, you are probably frustrating the child, even though your effort is genuine in trying to help. It works best to give the child one point on which to focus before beginning to play, praise him upon completion for achieving that particular goal, and add the other points needed when the time is ripe. Parents and teachers can almost always improve themselves in this area. Through improvement you are not only gaining better playing results, but more positive attitudes as well.

Do you talk a great deal to achieve your teaching results?
In the Suzuki method we are taught to teach by demonstration. If we are working to achieve all our results verbally, then we are not really teaching as true Suzuki teachers. We must constantly strive to improve ourselves in this area and teach by demonstrating on the instrument for the child.

Do you include specific instructions in the lesson for home practice?
It is easy to be general in our comments about home practice with statements such as "This is improving. Keep practicing." We can be much more effective when we become specific with our requests. For example, give comments such as: "I want you and mother to play this section 10 times a day this week. Five of those times I want you to play it very slowly (perhaps suggest a metronome setting for slow) and then gradually build your tempo the remaining five times (give those metronome settings also)." Guidance such as this leaves no uncertainty as to how the section should be practiced. Children and parents feel confident and practice more effectively when they know exactly what is expected of them.

Are you spending time with the reading assignment every lesson, once it is begun?

Beginning reading adds a new challenge to the piano lesson as well as to the home practice. It is difficult to fit it into the lesson time. However, it is necessary that it be done. It is wrong to assume that parent and child will continue their reading at home unless you are checking it in the lesson. Try doing it first in the lesson. Our Suzuki students must learn to read!

Are you teaching every note of each piece to your student?

If you are teaching every note of each piece, then you are missing part of the joy of Suzuki teaching. If you help train the children's parents to teach the notes in the beginning stages of the lessons, then you are free to deal with the musical ideas and new techniques in the lesson. This is not to say that you cannot help with certain notes and passages when they prove to be frustrating for the parent to handle. However, for the most part, if parents can do this at home, then you have time to draw the beautiful musical results from the child in the lesson.

Are your parents attentive and taking part in the child's lesson?

Since parents must implement our ideas in the home practice, it is imperative that they be attentive in the lesson. Be sure they are seated where they not only can hear, but see as well. Ask that they take notes. Involve them as much as possible in order to ascertain that they are developing the musical taste, understanding and refinement of the ear needed to be effective at home. For example, by involving them in listening activities in the lesson and asking their opinion on the tone quality, tempo, *etc.,* we keep their interest and attention and help to develop a sense of confidence in them that enables them to practice more effectively with their children at home.

Are you following the order of the Suzuki literature as you teach?

The Suzuki volumes have a carefully planned sequence of literature. Certain difficult pieces are inserted periodically to build skills. Often they are followed by easier ones to provide psychological relief. A teacher who skips to the easiest pieces is denying her student the chance to build the technique and skills which the more difficult pieces provide.

Are you completely honest in your statements to your students?

Children respect honesty. In seeking to praise, we can sometimes be dishonest. For instance, if the child plays poorly, many well-meaning teachers might tell him "good" when he finishes to make him feel better. Let us all continue to work to be positive, but perhaps if we strive to praise more specifically instead of generally, we can also be honest. For instance, in the case of a poor performance, perhaps we can tell the child how proud we were of him for continuing to play when things weren't going well. Add a bit of understanding with a statement such as "I have times when I don't play my best, either." Thus we have emphasized a positive element, shown understanding, and have been completely honest as well. In this way, you will command the child's respect, love, and trust in you.

Do you have Book 1 on the piano for the child while teaching, using it as a reference?

If you are teaching Book 1 to the child by referring to the music in the score, then you are teaching him as a traditional teacher would. In the beginning, we must constantly teach the child through sound, using no reference to the score. Later, when you have established your initial goals such as good tone and posture, then you can begin to call attention to the score in order to merge these skills into the reading.

Does your student constantly hesitate to find the big left hand jump in the last line of Allegretto 1 *before playing it?*

When the student first learns the big jump in *Allegretto 1*, it is a good opportunity to use the "stop-prepare" technique. However, once the child has his hands together comfortably on the piece, one of the goals in mastering it is to be able to play that difficult part smoothly, which includes maintaining a steady tempo throughout the phrase. This might involve your assigning many extra repetitions on that section in order to achieve a fine result.

Does the right hand maintain a nice legato at the end of line two of the Book 1 Musette?

The last two measures of line two of *Musette* are difficult. Before it can be considered a polished piece the right hand needs to maintain a smooth legato, even though the child might be detaching the left hand notes. Independence of the hands is needed to continue in the repertoire, so some extra repetitions to achieve it here will pay off in the volumes ahead.

Do your students maintain the same tempo on Chant Arabe between the A and B sections?

Chant Arabe is a sectional piece in which all of us tend to practice the A and B sections separately for quite a while when first learning it. This is good, but it is also important to make certain that the two sections maintain the same tempo when the piece is played as a whole. Most students tend to change tempo when going from one part to another.

Are you listening to tapes and recordings of the Suzuki literature?

Listening can be as valuable to the parent and teacher as it can to the student. I have grown tremendously as a musician through increased listening. Listening to the great artists helps to keep us elevated above the level of our students' playing. Consequently, we are always striving toward higher and higher goals for them.

Afterword

Throughout this book you have been given countless examples of ideas and techniques on how to achieve results in your teaching. Many of the ideas have been projected through dialogue because I have found that this enables the reader to visualize more precisely how a technique is implemented and consequently brings it to life for him. It has been a pleasure to use names of my own students in the dialogue.

If you have found even one new thought on which you feel you can grow, then the book has been well worth my efforts. If you have found a number of areas you would like to incorporate in your teaching, then I would like to make a suggestion: Try using the Suzuki one-point focus in doing so. First, make a list of the points you wish to implement. Place your list in an accessible place. Then, read your list at the beginning of each week and decide upon one point on which to focus in your teaching for the week. Repeat the same process the following week. Continue until you have achieved all the goals on your list.

I have learned to use the one-point focus in goals I have set for myself even outside of teaching and have been elated with the results. What used to seem overwhelming is no longer when it is accomplished one step at a time. I find it fascinating how this, as well as many of the basic elements of the Suzuki philosophy and techniques, can be applicable to our entire life.

It is my hope that you will not only grow from having read *Focus on Suzuki Piano*, but that it will additionally stimulate you toward new thoughts of your own. All of us must continue studying, thinking, growing, giving, and loving. In doing so, we are directing our own lives and minds toward being essential, vital, and beautiful human beings. In this way we are contributing toward and making a reality of the goals of peace, beauty, and love that Dr. Suzuki seeks for us.

Fine